HOPE
and
HEALINGS

Be blessed and encouraged.
With love in Him.

Claudine Bray

Ps 91 : 1-2
Heb 11 : 1 and 6

HOPE
and
HEALINGS

my true story

Claudine Bray

Claudine Bray

EVANGELISTA MEDIA™ srl
Via Maiella, 1
66020 San Giovanni Teatino (Ch) – Italy

"Changing the World, One Book at a Time."

This book and all other Evangelista Media™ and Destiny Image™ Europe books are available at Christian bookstores and distributors worldwide.

To order products, or for any other correspondence:

EVANGELISTA MEDIA™ srl
Via della Scafa, 29/14
65013 Città Sant'Angelo – Italy
Tel. +39 085 4716623 • Fax: +39 085 9090113
Email: info@evangelistamedia.com

Or reach us on the Internet: www.evangelistamedia.com

ISBN 13: 978-88-97896-47-0
ISBN 13 EBOOK: 978-88-97896-49-4

For Worldwide Distribution, Printed in the U.S.A.
1 2 3 4 5 6 / 16 15 14 13

ENDORSEMENTS

Claudine Bray is a woman who testifies to miraculous healings in her life. In her book *Hope and Healings*, you will read an account of a woman who dared to believe that God is good and that His promises to her never fail. A compelling and inspiring read!

Shirley Brownhill
Founder of Youth With A Mission
Perth, Australia

Claudine has documented here a remarkable journey from serious illness related to a brain tumor with many setbacks on the way to sustained health. What shines in her story is Claudine's unshakable faith and religious devotion which supported and encouraged her through several relapses. Her absolute trust in God and His healing powers is core to her remarkable recovery. Claudine's current vibrant health attests to the long-lasting nature of her recovery. You will be inspired by reading the account of her healing.

Dr. Anthony Keller, MB, BS, FRACP
Immunologist and Transfusion Medicine Specialist
Perth, Australia

As a follower of Jesus Christ, Claudine passionately believes that His coming inaugurated the kingdom of God on earth. And as we live between the commencement and the consummation of that kingdom, there are occasional moments of grace in which we experience a taste of God's purpose to restore all things one day. Healings are examples of such moments, and Claudine has been blessed to be the recipient of such grace. Read this story and be encouraged.

Dr. Haydn D. Nelson
Senior Minister, Riverview Church
Perth, Australia

CONTENTS

FOREWORD

Divine healing is unquestionably a part of the atonement that Jesus Christ made on the Cross of Calvary according to Isaiah 53:4-5 (NKJV) which reads: "Surely He [Jesus] has borne our griefs [lit., sicknesses] and carried our sorrows [lit., pains]; yet we esteemed Him stricken, smitten by God, and afflicted. But He was wounded for our transgressions, He was bruised for our iniquities; the chastisement for our peace was upon Him, and by His stripes we are healed."

Five times the word "our" is used, emphasizing that Jesus died in our place, to redeem us from our sin and sickness and death. Isaiah, moved by the Holy Spirit, recorded that prophecy over 700 years before Christ was born. Matthew records how that prophecy was fulfilled: "...And He cast out the spirits with a word, and healed all who were sick, that it might be fulfilled which was spoken by Isaiah the prophet saying: 'He Himself took our infirmities and bore our sicknesses'" (Matthew 8:16-17 NKJV).

Down through the years of our ministry, we have seen God do many wonderful miracles of healing, and not only through those who have been recognized as having the gift of healing, but also believers who have taken God at His word, and prayed according to Mark 16:17-18 (NKJV), "And these signs will follow those who believe: In My name they will cast out demons; they will speak with new tongues...they will lay hands on the sick, and they will recover."

However, we must also acknowledge, that there are many people who have been afflicted with various diseases and sicknesses who have not received healing when they have been prayed for. Even the great Charles Price, author of *The Real Faith*, whom God used mightily in healing crusades in the early 1900s and who saw great miracles including people getting out of wheelchairs, used to go back to his home or hotel after these great meetings and weep into the night for those who were not healed and who were not raised from their wheelchairs.

In writing the Foreword to this book, I felt it needful to lay the foundation for our faith in Christ and His Word; because whether we see healing or not, we must remember that God is faithful to His Word, and that He has many ways of bringing His Word to pass. In the case of our dear friend Claudine Bray, healing didn't come immediately, but eventually; and though she suffered quite considerably in the meantime, she experienced revelations and encouragements from the Lord that certainly enriched her life.

I am reminded of Job (don't we so often refer to him as an illustration?); he had a testimony from God that he was a blameless and upright man, one who feared God, and shunned evil. And yet he went through a severe testing time, to the point where Job said, "Though He slay me, yet will I trust Him..." (Job 13:15 NKJV). What an incredible statement for him to make! What an incredible faith he had in his God, regardless of his suffering. And finally Job's faith was rewarded, and God restored his losses, and gave him twice as much as he had before, "Now the Lord blessed the latter days of Job more than his beginning..." (Job 42:12 NKJV).

And so in commending this book to you, I know that you will be enriched and blessed as Claudine walks you through her incredible journey. My prayer is that you will become a faithful and true worshiper of God as she has, all because she never turned back from trusting and following her God, knowing that whatever happened, God would bring her through. Though it was not a pleasant experience, she is the richer for it.

Be blessed,

Pastor (Retired) Fred Anderson
Hillside Church
Forrestfield, Australia

PREFACE

First of all let me tell you, dear reader, who I am. Born in France, I have one sister, and we were brought up as Catholics. We attended church regularly on Sundays and lessons in catechism once a week. We were taught and had to memorize many statements such as: *Où est Dieu? Dieu rest partout, au ciel, sur la terre et en Tous lieux*, which, in English, means: Where is God? God is everywhere, in Heaven, on the earth, and in all places.

During the mass, the priest would preach a message related to a chosen passage of the Bible, which was written on the missal that everyone received when they took their first Communion at the age of 12, one year before receiving the Holy Spirit at their confirmation. Such was the tradition of the Catholic religion.

Being a believer did not have much impact at all on my lifestyle here on earth; and in my teenage years, I did not attend church regularly. However I clearly remember always saying my prayer at night before falling asleep. My focus for my future was to become an English teacher in France. During my seven years at secondary school, I started practicing English by spending several weeks of my summer holidays on the Isle of Wight.

Then, after studying for two years at the University of Caen, I was appointed as a French assistant at Dorking County Grammar School in Surrey and later on at Polytechnics of the South Bank in London, which is now known as London University of the South Bank. At that time I met several English friends with whom I am still in contact today.

In 1974 I met in Epsom my husband-to-be, Mike, who was Australian. Our wedding took place in France in 1975, and we lived in England until Christmas 1976 when we moved to Perth.

After we had settled in Australia, we decided to return to church by attending the Anglican church on one Sunday and the Catholic church the following week. We enjoyed doing this regularly for a few years but did not experience any change at all in our lifestyle until one of my husband's clients introduced us to Inner City Faith Church in Perth. That church was very different from ours, filled with many members who were always full of joy as they were singing amazing songs of praise and worship before hearing an encouraging message that explained how, by believing in God, we can have a much better life here on earth and we also have eternal life after we die. Home fellowships were organized in private houses during the week; and to learn more about the words written in the Bible, a Bible college was open during the week. At that time in my life, I started not only to know about God but especially to have a personal relationship with Him.

I really enjoyed living in Australia which, despite its isolation in the world, has advantages such as a wonderful sunny weather for most of the year, many beautiful places to visit, and a very relaxing lifestyle. Once every four years, my husband and I and our two lovely daughters, Nadége and Annabelle, visited all my relatives in France.

The number of my students kept increasing over the years, and I felt more and more fulfilled in my career. I was also thrilled that our two daughters had begun successful careers, and at the end of 1998, they had secure futures awaiting them.

However, from that time onward, I experienced the fact that no one can rely on what he or she has at the moment—whether it relates to health or finances. Very unexpectedly a total change can happen in anyone's life, as it did in mine. I started living by faith and not by sight, declaring that everything was going to turn into good.

My story, which has a very painful beginning in 1998, finishes in 2009 with a victory, a victory that continues today.

❁ ❁ ❁

Hope and perseverance are what everyone needs in times of difficult and very unexpected challenges. The purpose of this book is to bring you a totally new way of looking at life—the best way to confront trials whether health, financial, or any other area you are facing.

Based on my own experiences, I can truly say to you, "Don't let yourself become discouraged; instead, see yourself already as a winner—as a victor and not a victim, one who will become stronger than ever before. The harder your test, the more empow-ered you will become."

I hope you enjoy reading this book, and I sincerely hope that you will adopt a new outlook on life—one of success and strength, hope and healing.

With love in Christ,
Claudine

1

1998—HOW IT SUDDENLY BEGAN

1

1998—HOW IT SUDDENLY BEGAN

..."*This sickness will not end in death. No, it is for God's glory so that God's Son may be glorified through it*" (John 11:4 NIV).

During the last week in June 1998, I had the flu. I recovered in July. One Sunday, after spending quite a long time with one of my neighbors, as I stood up, I suddenly lost control of my balance. My husband was called, and he came to fetch me by car. I went straight to bed and did not eat much for dinner. Later that evening, my husband and I prayed, asking God and also thanking Him for healing my body of what was suddenly affecting it.

The following day, however, I still could not control my walking. I had to shuffle and stagger to go to the bathroom. Having lost my physical abilities, I stayed in bed most of the time, reading my Bible. God was my only rescue, the only One who was comforting me by

His Word, by being my "refuge and strength, an ever-present help in trouble" (Psalm 46:1 NIV).

At this time in my life, I felt as if my entire being was sapped of all energy and stamina. This trial started very suddenly during the time when I, thankfully, no longer had to drive or pick up our two daughters from school. I also had more freedom to organize my private language classes. The thought of being able to lead a more stress-free and enjoyable life was replaced with having to stay at home lying in bed or sitting in a chair. Most physical activity was beyond my capability.

My doctor sent me under observation to Royal Perth Hospital where the result of a CT scan of the brain showed no abnormality. Such a report sounded very positive but did not manifest as being correct because I did not regain my ability to walk. The medical team did no further investigative tests, which really disappointed me. I was morally hurt and physically weak, but spiritually I was strong. I was very disappointed to realize that doctors did not believe me when I described my symptoms, so I turned my eyes more and more toward Jesus, the only One who was giving me hope.

When I returned home two weeks later, I was still unable to lift up my feet but, although my life was very affected in the physical, I kept confessing and believing that all our sicknesses had been taken away by the death of Jesus on the Cross and that none of us was meant to be sick. Every day I confessed my faith in God and thanked Him for enabling me to live normally again.

The answer to my prayers came into pass in the middle of August, about the time when I was to start teaching again. To my greatest surprise, suddenly one day, I heard a voice saying that I "should have a private medical cover." I really did not understand the reason of that request that was definitely contradicting my faith in God's healing power. However, although I could not understand why, I obeyed the voice I had heard. I believed that the Holy Spirit, my Friend and my Helper, was at that precise moment showing Himself as my Guide and Counselor for my future.

On September 7 and 8 in 1998, I was given two prophecies by the prophet Fergus McIntyre. In the first one, which was very short, he said: "A merry heart is good like a medicine, isn't it? …It's like taking a medicine…Thank you Father…More medicine, more medicine. Give her the bottle. She is taking three teaspoons, but make her have buckets of it…Buckets of it, buckets of it, buckets of it." I definitely was not encouraged by these words. I did not want to believe in them, and I put them out of my thoughts.

The content of the second prophecy was totally different. This one was quite long and very encouraging by statements such as: "God gives you His love, His grace, His mercy, and His favor. I see you sitting on God's knees…and God is just talking to you, just loving you, just enjoying you…There is joy, there is joy coming…God's Spirit is going to spoil you…God is saying, 'Don't look into the past. Look into the future' …God is taking you into great places. In one year from now, I tell you, you are going to see some of the things that have been spoken to you tonight."

I was really touched by this prophecy. I was thrilled, looking forward to my future, especially to the coming year. However, a few weeks later my anticipated joy in God's plans for my life was totally wiped out when I had a relapse.

This is how it happened:

In the morning of Tuesday, October 13, I woke up feeling great, looking forward to my day. I attended the Bible college for the first lesson of the fourth term. Afterward, as I was driving to one of my students' home in Subiaco, I suddenly had blurred vision. I was seeing a lot of dots instead of a clear picture of the road. I had to park my car along the pavement where I waited for one and a half hours before my sight became clear again. Then I slowly drove back home where I went to bed as soon as I arrived. I had a good night's sleep, but the following morning I again shuffled and staggered as soon as I got up and tried to walk. I completely lost my appetite and the only drink I could take was apple juice. As I was not consuming any solids but only drinking, my health deteriorated quickly over the next few weeks. I lost weight, and my body became bony at the end of October, two weeks after my relapse started. My physical appearance and the experience I was going through were similar to Job's:

> *...on a bed of pain with constant distress in their bones, so that their body finds food repulsive and their soul loathes the choicest meal. Their flesh wastes away to nothing, and their bones, once hidden, now stick out* (Job 33:19-21 NIV).

At that stage, although I was physically weak, my trust in God and my faith in being healed were so strong that instead of going to see my doctor, I kept on praying, confessing my faith in God, and already thanking Jesus for restoring me. However, on October 27, I vomited as soon as I got up, and my husband finally drove me to the medical center. From there I was sent to Armadale Hospital where my doctor visited on a daily basis.

HOPEFUL

The Armadale Hospital doctor examined my eyes several times a day but never detected any abnormality. She often reminded me that the CT scan done in July was normal. I was praying regularly, asking God to show the doctor the cause of my blurred vision, which was becoming more frequent but unfortunately never in front of her.

The day before I was supposed to be discharged, I was feeling much better. That morning as I was sitting on a chair chatting with the other patients and a nurse, my prayer was answered that someone would diagnose my blurred vision. As we chatted, my vision suddenly became blurred. The nurse made me lie down on the bed. She examined my eyes with a light and looking very anxious, she left the ward and came back not long afterward with a hospital doctor who examined my eyes. Then she looked at the nurse and said, "Yes, Chris. She's got it." I did not have the faintest idea what those words meant. The only thing I was told was that, the following day, I would be driven by ambulance to Saint John of God Hospital in Murdoch for an MRI (Magnetic Resonance Imaging) of my brain.

The MRI took quite a long time, and some tests had to be done several times. My weight had dropped to 40 kilos (88 pounds), and when I got up that evening my walking was very, very slow. I can still remember how I said to myself, *I hope that tomorrow will be better.* I was physically very weak—but in the spiritual, and as much as possible in the natural, I was full of joy. Not only had my prayer been answered, but the fulfillment of one of the prophecies received a few weeks before was coming into pass. I decided from then onward to rely on the very encouraging words of the other prophecy, which brought me more *confidence* for my future. Although I could not perceive, not even imagine how this healing was possible, I reached a higher level of faith for total restoration and healing. I confessed that whatever abnormality I had would not be too hard for God to fix because with Him nothing, nothing is impossible, "For nothing is impossible with God" (Luke 1:37).

A VISION

During the first few hours of the night after I had the MRI, I was morally relieved: soon the doctors would know exactly what was affecting me. I fell asleep very hopeful. However, I was suddenly awakened at 4:30 a.m. by a horrible vision: my doctor standing up in front of my husband and saying to him: "What your wife has is very serious. It's a…" This last word left me in the unknown. I spoke to the Holy Spirit and asked Him to strengthen me and to prepare me to hear the end of this statement a few hours later.

After such a vision, as soon as I opened my eyes I started sobbing. I was then in total despair, unable to move my legs. I called the nurse who could hardly raise them. She tried to encourage me by saying that I would feel better later on. However, as she was saying these words, she looked anxious and slight tears appeared in her eyes.

Experiencing paralysis in my legs prepared me to hear the results of the MRI by my doctor. As soon as my husband arrived at 9 o'clock, I said to him that the news would not be encouraging at all. Later on when the doctor entered in the ward, looking at my husband, he said, "What your wife has is very serious. It's a brain tumor." Then he looked at me and added, "From now on there is no point for you to stay here. You will have to go to Sir Charles Gairdner Hospital, which has much better equipment and specialists in the treatment of cancers and tumors."

My doctor, my husband, and I were not only shocked but also devastated. It was hard to understand how such a serious condition had manifested itself so suddenly and in such an unexpected way. The Holy Spirit helped me to be brave to accept this bad report without showing any of my emotions to the doctor; but as soon as he left the room, I burst into tears. This news was for me the confirmation of being totally dependent on God. I put myself in His hands and relied on Him. With all my *trust* in Him, I decided then to be anointed with oil the following day.

I will always remember how I was released from Armadale Hospital on Sunday, November 8. My husband pushing me to the car in a wheelchair—a situation I never thought I would experience. When we arrived at church so I could be anointed, I was pleased to find myself again in a Christian atmosphere, surrounded by people worshiping the Lord. Emotionally, I was thrilled. Physically, I was not well at all on that day; my head was bent down, I was holding a bowl on my lap, feeling like vomiting, and I had horrible pains in my stomach. Spiritually, I was pleased to be obeying the Word of God that says:

> *Are any of you sick? You should call for the **elders of the church** to come and pray over you, anointing you with oil in the name of the Lord. Such a prayer offered in faith will heal the sick, and the Lord will make you well. And if you have committed any sins, you will be forgiven* (James 5:14-15).

I vividly remember also how people were "shocked" by seeing how my health had deteriorated so quickly. I can also remember the pastor announcing that I had a brain tumor that might be inoperable. Then he gave me a hug, saying: "Be strong, Claudine. God has already done many good things in your life. He can do it again, and then you will be a good witness of Him to everyone." Such a statement had a big impact on me. I was hearing the confirmation of what had been prophesied to me a few months before.

From then onward my hope, trust, and total confidence in God increased—in God, the One in charge of our lives who has a plan for our futures; as it is written in the book of Jeremiah:

"For I know the plans I have for you," says the Lord. "They are plans for good and not for disaster, to give you a future and a hope" (Jeremiah 29:11).

Throughout the book I have included Scripture passages that brought me hope and encouragement; I share them with you believing that you too will be comforted:

The grave wrapped its ropes around me; death laid a trap in my path. But in my distress I cried out to the Lord; yes, I prayed to my God for help. He heard me from his sanctuary; my cry to him reached his ears (Psalm 18:5-6).

AT THE SIR CHARLES GAIRDNER HOSPITAL

On Tuesday, November 10, 1998, my husband drove me to the neurological clinic before I was admitted to the hospital. One doctor examined me and asked if my daughters knew that I had a brain tumor. I answered that I had told them the truth and, with relief, she said, "I am pleased you did. It is wise for them to know."

It really looked as if satan was going to win the battle. However, I was determined to keep on confessing that I was not yet at the end of my life. Satan had taken my health, but he was not going to take my life. At that stage I was saying to satan the words that God had spoken to him about Job: "'All right, do with him as you please' the Lord said to Satan. 'But spare his life'" (Job 2:6). Although I could not understand the reason for my sickness, although I was shattered by such a rapid change in my health, I reminded myself that God's thoughts and ways of acting are very different—but much better than ours. He has a plan for each one's life, which shows that "all things work together for good to those who love God, to those who are called according to His purpose" (Romans 8:28 NKJV).

During my first night at Sir Charles Gairdner, I heard the voice of the Holy Spirit saying very clearly that "it is impossible to please God without faith" (Hebrews 11:6). As my greatest desire was to please Him more than ever, these words really increased my faith—although I could not imagine at all how this could ever take place.

❖◌❖◌❖◌❖◌❖◌❖◌❖◌❖◌❖◌❖◌❖

As my greatest desire was to please Him more than ever,
the words in Hebrews 11:6 greatly increased my faith.

❖◌❖◌❖◌❖◌❖◌❖◌❖◌❖◌❖◌❖◌❖

Physically, not only was I in agony, but also in real darkness, feeling abandoned and so lonely that I asked the nurse to call my husband and my daughter Nadége. I suddenly felt such atrocious pains that fear invaded me. My flesh was very tight from the level of my hips to the top of my abdomen. Quite often I had strong contractions on the left side. It was as if a snake was crawling and biting my flesh for quite a long time before suddenly releasing it.

Then I could cope for a while until the unbearable pain manifested itself again.

I could no longer utter any words. The only way I communicated with God was by speaking in tongues. At that stage, my body must have looked incredibly tortured to the eyes of those around me, even the nurses. The first morning I woke up at hospital one of the nurses came early to ask me the name of my church and pastor, whom she called straightaway.

TWO MORE VISIONS

At that time I had two visions. Very often I was seeing myself in a very long, dark tunnel at the end of which, one day, I would see the light. Occasionally, I was in dark clouds which, at God's appointed time, would totally fade away and be replaced by a beautiful sun. These two visions brought me hope and faith for my future.

I believed more and more that the Holy Spirit was going to keep strengthening me in difficult times.

I compared myself to a soldier fighting in times of war, falling fairly often on the ground, but always able to rise again and finally win the battle. I was very encouraged by reading the following Scripture:

> ...*For though I fall, I will rise again. Though I sit in darkness, the Lord will be my light* (Micah 7:8).

The results of sickness and pain were illustrated by several points in my spiritual life. My only desire at that time was to be closer to God and to please Him more than I ever had before. To achieve this I decided:

1. To ask God for forgiveness of whatever sins I had committed, full of regrets for not having always remembered Him enough, loved Him, and pleased Him as I should have.

2. To accept God's forgiveness and forget completely my mistakes in the past.

3. To forgive those who had hurt me in the past.

4. To love everyone I knew.

5. To love God more and more.

Turning my eyes upon the Lord was my only rescue. I was determined not to let myself be affected by my physical feelings and what I looked like. I was very encouraged by the following words of God:

> *Don't be afraid, for I am with you. **Don't be discouraged,** for I am your God. **I will strengthen you and help you. I will hold you up with my victorious right hand** (Isaiah 41:10).*

On my second day in the hospital I had a scan of all the bones from the bottom of my feet to the top of my head. I cried out to God, asking Him to comfort me, to enable me to cope with the atrocious pain I was feeling from my hips to my upper stomach.

Everything was at its worse when the tests started. However, I was suddenly amazed by a wonderful vision. I saw myself in Heaven with angels dressed up in very shining, sparkling, and glittering white clothes. They were forming half a circle, welcoming all the people entering into Heaven. Surrounded by wonderful bright lights, these angels were in front of a golden door.

Such a sight of our entry into Heaven was really beautiful; but I cannot say anymore about it because as soon as the machine was over my head, I started living again in the physical, feeling again my body, which was still in agony.

FROM THEN UNTIL NOW

Since the beginning of my relapse in the month of October, I had now been sick at home for two weeks, at Armadale Hospital for two weeks, and it was now the end of my first week at Sir Charles Gairdner—one week during which my pains had become more and more unbearable. I continually confessed and thanked God as my Healer through His Son Jesus who suffered and died for all of us.

Several churches had been praying for me, but there was no sign of improvement. On the contrary, my pain was so continuous that my faith began to waver. The thought of being in Heaven came to my mind, and I had a vision of Jesus holding me on His lap and speaking to me words of encouragement, which were the illustration of one prophecy received at the Bible college in September, two months earlier. It would have been so much better to enjoy eternal life with Him than live in pain on earth. My strong desire to be absent from the body and present with the Lord became my way of looking at life (see 1 Cor. 5:3; 2 Cor. 5:8).

AN OUT-OF-BODY EXPERIENCE

The place in which I was living during this time was similar to a cloud from where my eyes could look down at the world and at the people I knew. I could see more and more of them at church, raising their arms during the time of praise and worship. My perception of Perth was no longer the same. I knew that Perth was a wonderful city, but the only parts I could remember included its wide river full of blue and smooth water for most of the year, a long and very wide bridge, and a freeway on which I had enjoyed driving so many times. All these pictures, which I had truly seen in the past, could not be compared to the serene and peaceful places in which I was now. I was no longer grieving the loss of my health for the joy of the Lord was my strength. Turning my eyes upon Him increased my joy and strength every day; and by giving myself fully to Him, I could feel His presence more and more deeply.

Love is what *leads* over victorious expectations!

*Love **never** fails* (1 Corinthians 13:8 NIV).

Confess that *fear is the opposite of faith.*

Do not FEAR—do not have any False Expectations Appearing Real. Instead of fear, **have JOY** by showing Jesus On You.

When you face health problems, always remember to:

1. Have faith in God as your Healer

2. Have determination in seeing sickness as temporary—but health as being eternal.

3. Surrender to God and trust Him.

4. Live one day at a time, full of spiritual joy.

My Faith Revived

When I tried to imagine what my husband—and even more my daughters' lives—would be like if death took me away, I suddenly remembered the words that I had clearly heard from God, which came from Hebrews 11:6, "And it is impossible to please God without faith. Anyone who wants to come to Him must believe that God exists and that He rewards those who sincerely seek Him."

As my greatest desire was to please God, my faith in being healed was revived—even though I could not imagine how it would take place. At the moment when I made that decision, I heard a very, very soft voice saying, "Be still...be still...be still, and know that I am God" (Psalm 46:10). These words became some of my favorite ones, and anxiety left me completely. My faith and hope rose again.

My trust in God increased, and worship started playing a big part in my life since most of the Scriptures that were very encouraging to me were all turned into songs such as Psalm 91:1-2 (NKJV), which I had read while I was at my greatest despair:

He who dwells in the secret place
of the Most High
shall abide under the shadow of the Almighty.
I will say of the Lord:
"He is my refuge and my fortress;
my God, in Him I will trust."

I encouraged myself by listening, during the day and sometimes at night, to tapes of worship and to healing Scriptures read by Pastor Benny Hinn. I was living on a daily basis, never thinking about tomorrow. My two favorite songs were entitled, "One Day at a Time" and "Be Still and Know that I Am God." Other songs such as "The Joy of the Lord," "You Are the Lord Who Heals Me," "Rise and be Healed," and one CD entitled "Atmosphere for Healing" also encouraged me and changed me completely by enabling me to feel closer to God.

Although I was still in pain, my outlook on life was no longer the same. I wanted to please God by having faith in Him as my Healer. I was determined to keep on fighting the good fight of faith, to live and not to die. I was morally strengthened by having visitors, especially by seeing my husband, Mike, and our daughters, Nadége and Annabelle, on a daily basis. I had more and more the desire of coming back to earth with them, but only if I received a miraculous healing, only if I became able to walk again.

MY FAITH TESTED AGAIN

It was now the end of November 1998, and the pain in my abdomen had stopped. At the time when I had just started winning over my serious sickness, my faith was suddenly tested again.

Doctors were still doing tests on my body. A lumbar puncture, a very painful test, was done at the top of my spine. Afterward, I had to remain very still for a few hours in the afternoon. At 5 p.m., when dinner was served to all the patients, I believed that this medical test had been successful and, with confidence, I lifted up my body. Unfortunately, I suddenly felt a strong spasm in my neck. To find relief, I had to immediately lie down again; from then onward, every time I tried to lift up my neck, I felt strong and very painful spasms. As a result of this lumbar puncture—for a whole week—I was unable to eat any food without vomiting.

To prevent fear from invading me, I relied on this Scripture verse, "Yea, though I walk through the valley of the shadow of death, I will fear no evil: for thou art with me; thy rod and thy staff they comfort me" (Psalm 23:4 KJV). At that stage, I definitely knew that my days would not come to an end, and I declared that darkness in my life would not affect me as it had previously.

One day I was suddenly dumbfounded by seeing clearly the face of all my French relatives who had died many years ago, before I came to Australia. I remembered each one's name very clearly as soon as he or she appeared in front of my eyes. They all looked radiant with happy smiles. I was in ecstasy, thrilled to see all of them again. However I did not have any desire to go where they were now. My greatest desire was to stay alive and live a normal life again. I decided to rely on God by trusting Him more and more for my future.

The letters of the word TRUST are very powerful:

> *To have trust means to Truly and Totally*
> *Rest and Rely*
> *Upon*
> *Spiritual*
> *Teaching*

In December I was transferred into a different ward. The neurologist said that there was no connection between my brain tumor and the paralysis in my body. At the time when I did not have any more pain caused by my brain or by spasms in my neck, I was still unable to move my body. In the natural, I felt totally abandoned by the medical team who was saying that nothing could be done. Hearing such a statement made me feel heartbroken. However, spiritually, I was encouraged by remembering the words of Jesus, "Never will I leave you; never will I forsake you" (Hebrews 13:5 NIV).

One evening, my faith in being well was confirmed by a vision in which I saw myself driving on the freeway from Perth to the south of the river where I lived. This picture was so clear that, straightaway, I tried to lift up my legs. This was done in vain, but I had been so touched by the vision that I believed more and more that my dream would become true.

At the end of my fourth week in the hospital, I was allowed for the first time to be taken out for the day. My husband took me to church in a wheelchair. I was thrilled to fellowship with other people and to hear biblical teaching again. Unfortunately, that day I suddenly felt strong pains in my neck and at the back of my brain. In the afternoon, I felt like vomiting and lost my appetite. By 5 p.m. I was back at Sir Charles Gairdner Hospital.

In the evening I heard the Holy Spirit telling me that to receive my healing I had to make the first steps.

First Steps to Healing

As I was reading the book of Matthew, I felt as if Jesus was speaking to me by saying:

> *...if you have faith as small as a mustard seed, you can say to this mountain "Move from here to there," and it will move. **Nothing will be impossible for you*** (Matthew 17:20 NIV).

After hearing these words, I became more than ever determined to move my legs again. I was no longer prepared to stay alive unless I led a normal life.

I was strong in my faith; but having faith in God's healing power was not enough in itself because, as it says in James 2:26, "Faith is dead without good works." Therefore I decided to try to take my first steps. I slid my body across the mattress, put my legs on the floor, stood up behind the wheelchair, and tried to push it. My feet were shuffling, my steps were very small, and after I advanced a length of 2 meters (6 feet) at the very most, my back and legs became weak. So I quickly turned my chair toward me and sat in it.

I had put my faith into action by forcing myself to take a few steps. Then I spoke to God. I told Him that His Word does not say that "Nothing is impossible *to* God" but that "Nothing is impossible with God." Luke 18:27 says, "Jesus replied, "What is impossible for people *is possible with God*." As I had just made the effort of trying to walk, therefore I believed that from then onward God was going to help me receive total healing.

By having made these first few steps, I had done what He was expecting from me. I had just proved that my body did not belong to sickness but to the Holy Spirit whose desire was to see me in divine health. At that time, I was encouraged by remembering that our "sufferings of this present time are not worthy to be compared with the glory which shall be revealed in us" (Romans 8:18 NKJV). I rejected the fear of falling each time I tried to walk.

Some days my body would suddenly feel weak and then I had to use the wheelchair. However, instead of losing any hope, I kept declaring my faith and trust in God, thanking Him in advance for making me whole.

From one day to the next, not much change was visible in my physical abilities except the fact that I was becoming more confident and used the chair less and less.

FIGHTING FOR THE VICTORY

In the ward where I had been transferred, I was blessed by meeting Maggie, a lady who had several points in common with me:

1. She had been suffering from cancer for a few years.

2. She was spending most of her time in a wheelchair.

3. She believed in God whom she was praising and thanking every day for the healing she was expecting.

Both of us found joy through worship. Our favorite song was "The Joy of the Lord Is My Strength." We were living one day at a time, no longer looking at the past or at the future, but trying to enjoy the present as much as we could.

During the second week of December, my walking gradually improved, and a turning point happened on Sunday, December 13, when I forced myself to walk a much longer distance. For the first time I arrived at church without being in the wheelchair. Doing this was a real thrill and a real challenge for me. Unfortunately, my body had not yet regained all its strength. At the end of the service, I could not take any more steps and had to borrow a wheelchair.

During the following week the length of my walking gradually increased in the hospital and the wheelchair was no longer needed.

On Sunday, December 20, I arrived at and left from church walking! I was full of joy from finally witnessing God's divine power. Then on Tuesday, December 22, 1998, I was discharged from Sir Charles Gairdner Hospital. I was a walking miracle. God was glorified, and many were encouraged for their future.

After spending eight weeks in two different hospitals, I won the victory by:

1. Fighting the good fight of faith and seeing how faith and work (deeds) cannot be separated.

2. Taking the first steps after which God came to my rescue and healed me totally.

3. Seeing that God was in charge of my life. He had a plan for my future and turned my hard times into good.

Never forget that what God did upon me, He can also do upon anyone else. God loves everyone the same; but each person must start working on the impossible before seeing the miracle coming from God.

UPLIFTED BY THE WORD OF GOD

My focus was more on my relationship with God and on the supernatural than on the results of medical tests. I confessed that God was in charge of my life and that He was able to turn my battles into victories, to replace pains and tears by health and joy. I also believed that as it is expressed by the following words, He was always near to protect and comfort me:

Surely he will save you from the fowler's snare and from the deadly pestilence. He will cover you with his feathers, and under his wings you will find refuge... (Psalm 91:3-4 NIV).

Under God's wings, I was in such a cozy place, such a safe place that nobody except God could touch me. I felt protected and much better within myself knowing that satan could not attack me anymore.

Psalm 91 also strengthened me and filled me with hope when I read the relationship that God desires to have with each of His children:

Those who live in the shelter of the Most High will find rest in the shadow of the Almighty. This I declare about the

Lord: He alone is my refuge, my place of safety; he is my God, and I trust him (Psalm 91:1-2).

He will call on me, and I will answer him; I will be with him in trouble, I will deliver him and honor him. With long life I will satisfy him and show him my salvation (Psalm 91:15-16 NIV).

Other Scriptures that brought me hope and confidence for my future:

*Without faith it is impossible to **please God*** (Hebrews 11:6 NIV).

*Be still, and know that **I am God*** (Psalm 46:10 NIV).

*We do this by **keeping our eyes on Jesus**, the champion who initiates and perfects our faith* (Hebrews 12:2).

I am the Lord who heals you (Exodus 15:26).

*Even though I walk through the darkest valley, **I will fear no evil**, for you are with me* (Psalm 23:4 NIV).

*He was pierced for our transgressions, he was crushed for our iniquities; the punishment that brought us peace was on him, and by **his wounds we are healed*** (Isaiah 53:5 NIV).

God has not given us a spirit of fear**, but of **power** and of love and a **sound mind (2 Timothy 1:7 NKJV).

*When I fall, I will arise; when I sit in darkness, **the Lord will be a light to me*** (Micah 7:8 NKJV).

*Then God said, **"Let there be light,"** and there was light* (Genesis 1:3).

By experiencing sickness, I was in darkness; but I believed that one day I would see Light rising by receiving my healing. I had already fallen by becoming sick, but I was not going to lie down forever. Instead, I was going to rise up again, to be healed and become a witness of God's amazing mercy and grace.

POINTS TO PONDER

When faced with health, financial, family, or relationship issues:

- Ask God for forgiveness of whatever sins you have committed, full of regret for not having always remembered Him enough, loved Him, and pleased Him as you should have.

- Accept God's forgiveness and forget completely your mistakes in the past.

- Forgive those who have hurt you in the past.

- Love everyone you know.

- Love God more and more.

- Have faith in God as your Healer.

- Have determination in seeing sickness as temporary— but health as being eternal.

- Surrender to God and trust Him.

- Live one day at a time, full of spiritual joy.

Win your victory by:

- Fighting the good fight of faith and seeing how faith and work (deeds) cannot be separated.

- Taking the first steps after which God will come to rescue and heal you totally.

- Seeing that God is in charge of your life. He has a plan for your future and will turn your hard times into good.

2

1999—FACING HARD TIMES WITH FAITH

2
1999—FACING HARD TIMES WITH FAITH

The Lord is good, a refuge in times of trouble.
He cares for those who trust in him... (Nahum
1:7 NIV)

In the year 1999, my lifestyle changed completely. My health improved very slowly. I was gradually regaining all my physical abilities, but I had to show wisdom by not doing more than I was capable of.

Years follow one another and usually they are about the same with celebrations of birthdays and holidays, but suddenly one year can be totally different. This is exactly what I experienced in 1999. After teaching for an average of 18 hours a week the previous year, the number of my students dramatically reduced to ten in 1999 and then six the following year.

I still enjoyed tutoring, but my focus was no longer the same. Living in the spiritual realm was for me far more important than experiencing life such as it is in the natural. From the day I was released from hospital at the end of December 1998, I was spending most of my days at home, either outside on a deck chair or in the family room listening to tapes and CDs of praise and worship or watching Christian programs on television, especially "This Is Your Day" by Pastor Benny Hinn and "Enjoy Everyday Life" by Joyce Meyer.

My purpose in doing this was not only to hear the Word of God but also to glorify Him and encourage others.

On Sundays I regularly attended church with my husband, and during the week I was driving myself to church meetings to teach about healing. My purpose in doing this was not only to hear the Word of God but also to glorify Him and encourage others by witnessing how, in 1998, I had been so touched by Him.

Medically speaking, although I was recovering well, my brain had to be checked regularly. In February 1999, I had a second MRI of my brain after which I was told that the conditions looked stable.

I was far from doing as much as I had done in the past, but I was becoming stronger, which gave me the desire to visit my daughter in Melbourne. With godly wisdom, my husband and I decided that before making any airline reservations I should consult my doctor. He told me that flying would not be very wise because of the effect of the pressure on the brain. However, he allowed me to do so under the condition of reserving a seat on a jumbo airliner.

During our stay in Victoria, I felt very well and was thrilled to meet, for the first time, the family-in-law to-be of our daughter Annabelle who had been living in Melbourne for a few months. On the day of our return to Perth at the end of April 1999, I was still feeling very well during the flight. However a few days later, I had a relapse; and in the month of May, I had to be seen several times by a neurosurgeon.

Before I knew what I was facing, the neurologist and the neuro-surgeon discussed the results of the MRIs done in October 1998 and February 1999. When my husband and I saw the neurosurgeon, he told us that I didn't need a biopsy or a burr hole—I needed to have a craniotomy (surgery performed on the skull where a portion of bone is removed to gain access to the brain and the bone is put back in its place after the operation) that would be done in the left temporal lobe of my brain. The exact length of the operation could not be determined, nor could the result of a successful operation be guaranteed, for which I had to sign a release form.

PREPPING FOR THE SURGERY

At the beginning of June I had to spend one full day at the hospital for a general check-up. The following week, to give my body the resistance needed for the surgery, I was prescribed morphine. On Wednesday, June 9 at 10 o'clock in the morning, I arrived at Sir Charles Gairdner where I stayed in the observation ward until the middle of the afternoon.

At that point, as I was thinking about the experience I was facing. I cannot understand why, but suddenly I anticipated the possibility of becoming blind. That possibility really scared me. I was really frightened of what could be the result of this operation. By bringing fear upon me, satan was bringing a horrible thought in my mind, but I decided not to let this fear affect me for too long. I refused to live with this FEAR (False Expectation Appearing Real), and I replaced it by thanking the Holy Spirit for guiding the hands of the neurosurgeon. I knew that a craniotomy could have two totally different results. It would be successful if the neurosurgeon did not operate any lower than the level of my eyes. If not, I would become like a vegetable, losing all my abilities and even the consciousness of being alive.

❁✿❁✿❁✿❁✿❁✿❁✿❁✿❁✿❁✿❁✿❁✿❁

At that time I was totally in God's hands.
God was fully in control of the situation.

❁✿❁✿❁✿❁✿❁✿❁✿❁✿❁✿❁✿❁✿❁✿❁

As I was rejecting such a negative picture, I closed my eyes and turned them upon Jesus as a nurse pushed my bed into the operation theater at 3:30 p.m. At that time I was totally in God's hands. God was fully in control of the situation.

I believed and confessed that God was going to use the surgeon as an instrument of His healing power. I reminded myself of the following words:

The Lord is good, a strong refuge when trouble comes. He is close to those who trust in him (Nahum 1:7).

Do not fear, for I am with you; do not be dismayed, for I am your God. I will strengthen you and help you; I will uphold you with my righteous right hand (Isaiah 41:10 NIV).

Those who hope in the Lord will renew their strength. They will soar on wings like eagles; they will run and not grow weary; they will walk and not be faint (Isaiah 40:31 NIV).

My favorite and also most needed Scripture at that time was, "Be still, and know that I am God" (Psalm 46:10).

THE CRANIOTOMY AND THE AFTEREFFECTS

The craniotomy lasted for three and a half hours and they removed a piece of tissue which was 6 inches long. I cannot say how I felt in the operation theater or when I arrived or left the recovery ward. However, I clearly remember seeing two nurses and one doctor standing around my bed when I opened my eyes during the night. At that time I still had the oxygen mask on and the doctor was checking my eyes, my breathing, and blood pressure regularly. One of the nurses who had been called by emergency said to me that after giving me three lots of morphine in the space of a few hours to stop me from screaming, she, at last, no longer needed to give me more drugs because "finally" I was quiet.

When I woke up on the morning following the operation, I still remember how happy I was to see my daughter, Nadége, and my husband sitting near my bed. However I could not say much at all to them because I was still very tired from the ordeal. I was given a very light meal and was kept in the recovery ward until the afternoon. The day after the operation my physical appearance had totally changed. My left eye was bruised and my hair which used to be shoulder-length was now totally gone and replaced by a big bandage covering the left temporal lobe of my brain.

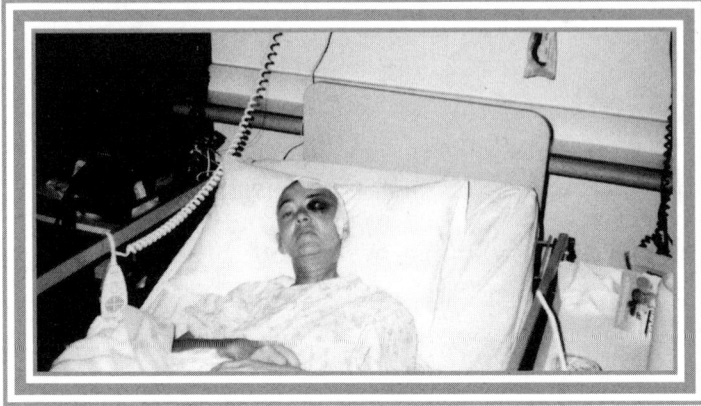

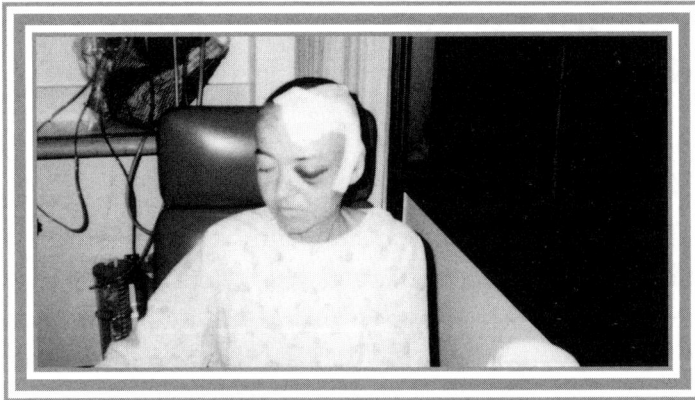

*Photos of me after the surgery
on June 10 and 11, 1999.*

Two days after the operation, I was asked to get up and sit in a chair close to the bed. Unfortunately, after only a short length of time, I became dizzy and had to lie down again. On Saturday, June 12, I was able to start walking, and a nurse took off the bandage and removed 28 stitches a few days later.

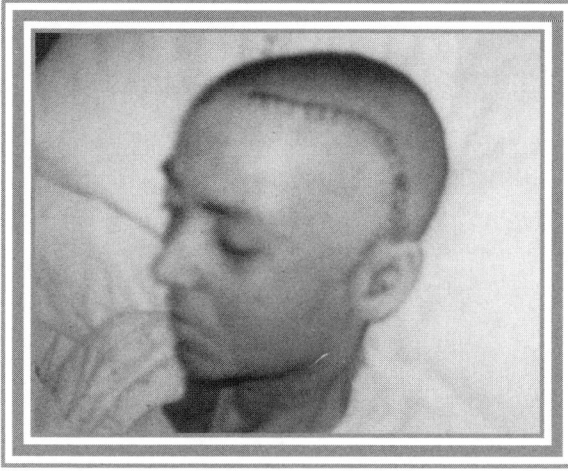

Amateur photo

Every day I slowly increased the length of my walking. I was living day by day, trying to do the best I could. The best encouragement was listening to praise and worship songs such as "One Day at a Time" and "The Joy of the Lord," which was the real strength I needed to fully recover.

After spending nearly two weeks at Sir Charles Gairdner Hospital, I returned home on Monday, June 21. I was not allowed to drive for eight weeks. I was confined at home until the beginning of August when I drove to see my doctor at his medical center. He was amazed to see how well I was recovering, and noticed that my hair changed color from dark brown to black.

AUGUST 1999

To keep track of the conditions in my brain, the doctor requested another MRI in August 1999 (my third since October 1998). From the middle of August on, I was able to gradually start teaching again and to attend meetings at church during the week and also services on Sunday. I was very thankful.

POINTS TO PONDER

Sometimes we just don't fully understand why things happen and we tend to worry about the future rather than knowing in our hearts and minds that God is in control of all things. The following are things you can do and ways to help you to focus on Jesus and His tender mercies:

- Read the Bible. Try reading from a different translation for new insights that the Holy Spirit may bring to your attention.
- Listen to Christian music.
- Watch Christian television shows or videos.
- Pray with your spouse or a friend.
- Read Christian novels or autobiographies of well-known Christians.
- Share your testimony with others.

Learn from yesterday, live for today, hope for tomorrow.

–Albert Einstein

When the world says, 'Give up,' Hope whispers, 'Try it one more time.'

–Author Unknown

Hope is that thing with feathers that perches in the soul and sings the tune without the words and never stops…at all.

–Emily Dickinson

Hope begins in the dark, the stubborn hope that if you just show up and try to do the right thing, the dawn will come.

–Anne Lamott

3

2000—WHAT I NEVER EXPECTED

3
2000—WHAT I NEVER EXPECTED

The Lord is my strength and shield. I trust him with all my heart. He helps me, and my heart is filled with joy... (Psalm 28:7).

The year 2000 started out good...until Monday, January 24. On that day I was feeling physically well when I got up and I was busy doing various things such as driving to accomplish errands, and walking to visit some of our neighbors. The day had been so hot that after dinner my husband and I decided to go for a drive. Many people were out that evening and, as it looked as if we would have to wait for a long time before being served in a café on the South bank of the river, we decided to drive along the esplanade in Perth. When we left the South of the river, I was walking normally. However, while my husband was driving over the bridge, I suddenly felt a slight throb in the left side of my brain.

When we arrived on the other side of the river, as soon as I got out of the car, I was shocked to realize that I could only walk very slowly. The size of my steps decreased so quickly that I had to sit down on a chair at a nearby table. After a short while, I felt that it would be wise for me to be medically checked. My husband drove me to Sir Charles Gairdner Hospital.

When we arrived, I was terrified when I realized that I was unable to get out of the car. I could no longer walk at all, and I had to use a wheelchair to get into the hospital. Several doctors examined me and said that I needed to have an MRI of the spine. After the medical examination, I was taken back to the car in a hospital wheelchair which, unfortunately, I could not borrow.

ANOTHER MRI

When I returned home, my steps were so small that it took me nearly 20 minutes to go from the front door to my bedroom. The following day when I got up, I could use neither my arms nor my legs. I had to sit on the floor and drag my body from my bed to the bathroom. From then on I lost all my physical abilities.

Upon waking each morning, my back looked normal except near my waist where there was (I quote from medical report) "a shallow central T11/12 disc herniation" of the spine (see photo 1). By early afternoon there was throbbing pain in my ribs. To find relief I had to lay down on my bed most of the afternoon. It was as if I was "being chastened on a bed of pain with constant distress on my bones" (see Job 33:19 NIV). At the end of each day (see photo 2), my whole back was in agony; my rib bones were sticking out like Job's whose bones "once hidden were now sticking out" (see Job 33:21 NIV). Before having such an experience, I would have never imagined that pain could be felt so strongly in my bones.

My body was affected by weakness in the muscles. I was ordered to have another MRI of my brain (my fourth since October 1998). The result was good. I was no longer suffering from the tumor in my brain, but satan was now attacking my spinal cord. A disc herniation of the spine was diagnosed.

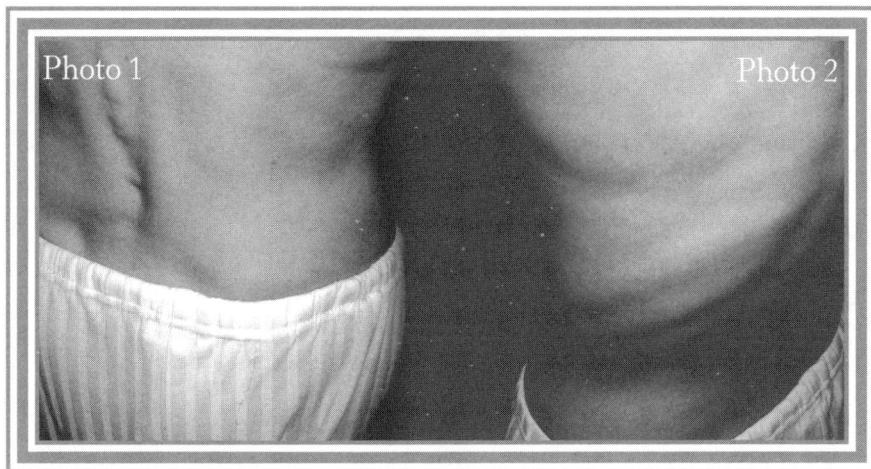

PHOTO 1: *What my back looked like at the beginning of each day—normal except at my spine where one disc had been pushed in.*

PHOTO 2: *What my back looked like at the end of each day when my ribs were sticking out.*

The surgeon did not want to risk such a serious operation of the spine, so I had to rent a wheelchair and was confined to it for mobility. My physical body was very affected, but I refused to let myself be emotionally or spiritually affected by this new trial. I refused to let satan take my joy away by confining me in my own house. Instead I relied on the following Scripture:

Consider it pure joy, my brothers and sisters, whenever you face trials of many kinds, because you know that the testing of your faith produces perseverance. Let perseverance finish its work so that you may be mature and complete, not lacking anything (James 1:2-4 NIV).

From then on I had very little choice in what I could do in my daily life. But instead of being trapped at home by myself, I decided to enjoy the summer weather by visiting some of my neighbors in my wheelchair. Every day my husband took me out for lunch, and sometimes I stayed for a few hours in a shopping center in my wheelchair.

So I could attend church conferences, a friend drove me. And during the first weekend of February, she drove me to a healing conference led by an American pastor. Several churches were praying for me, and on Friday evenings my husband drove me regularly to Youth With A Mission (YWAM). After each meeting, a friend drove me to a home fellowship where I joined my husband again.

"I WILL HEAL YOU"

Through such experiences, I discovered that all believers should be more thankful for the use of their arms and legs. We should never take anything for granted but rather appreciate how we have been created, recognizing how important each member of our body is for the leading of a normal life.

Because my physical activities were very limited, in order to be spiritually strengthened I decided to watch a Christian television program early every morning. The program entitled "This Is Your Day" was my favorite. I was, at that time, feeling weak in my body but strong in my spirit; and I was encouraged by hearing daily biblical teaching. I was motivated and inspired when I saw miracles happen. My personal expectations increased every time I saw people worshiping, and then suddenly being able to use their bodies normally again.

In the morning when I was waking up, although I could feel God's presence in me, quite often I would burst into tears because of all that I had been through. But one day I felt very encouraged by reading what God said to Hezekiah: "I have heard your prayer and seen your tears. I will heal you" (2 Kings 20:5).

I reminded myself very often that the promise made to Hezekiah was also meant to be mine, and I relied on it. Such a hope developed my trust in God. I looked more and more to Him and His mighty power. My favorite songs were "The Joy of the Lord," "The Potter's Hands," and "You Are the Lord Who Heals Me." However, the song that inspired me the most was "Rise and Be Healed" because all of the words illustrated what I needed and also expected to receive.

MY DIM FUTURE...BUT GOD...

Medically speaking, there was no possibility of total recovery. The only answer available for me to cope better with life was by spending some days at home and others in a hospice. Once more, God was my comfort, my refuge, and my hope as it is written in the following Scriptures:

> *I will say of the Lord, "He is my refuge and my fortress,*
> *my God, in whom I trust"* (Psalm 91:2 NIV).

Those who hope in the Lord will renew their strength. They will soar on wings like eagles; they will run and not grow weary, they will walk and not be faint (Isaiah 40:31).

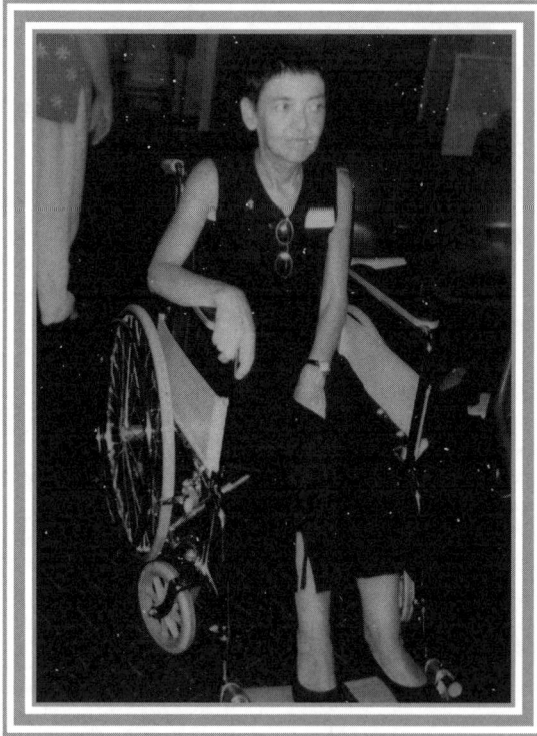

*I was confined to a wheelchair for five weeks,
before God healed me.*

On Thursday, February 24, 2000, at a weekly church meeting known as "Time for You," people prayed over me. One person, Frank, strongly rebuked satan. He declared that the wheelchair was not meant for me and that I was soon going to stop using it. He sounded so deeply convinced of his words that they were very powerful over me by increasing my hope and faith to a much higher level.

On Saturday, February 26, the day of my niece's wedding, I attended the ceremony in the wheelchair, which I felt was far from being a good witness of God to all my relatives.

The following morning, my husband and I attended Riverview Church, a church with a big congregation. I arrived in the wheelchair and I returned home in the wheelchair. Being booked on respite in a hospice in Murdoch for Monday, February 28, the last chance I had to receive my healing was by attending church in the afternoon at the Australasian Christian Fellowship, a small congregation that used to meet only once a month. A few months earlier at that place I had glorified God for the success of my craniotomy. Therefore, arriving in a wheelchair broke my heart since I was no longer witnessing a total recovery of my health.

When I arrived at that small church, I did not feel like speaking to anyone. So I turned the wheels of the chair as quickly as I could toward the doors of the building. As soon as I was inside, a strong anointing fell upon me. I felt that something very special was going to happen. I was full of expectancy, ready to receive a touch from God. In fact, I felt such an expectancy, after being in a wheelchair for five weeks, that for the first time I stood up and made a few steps during the praise and worship time. Unfortunately, I immediately felt pain and had to sit down again.

At the end of worship, the preacher stated that he had decided, not long before coming to church, that his message would be on healing. As I heard the word "healing," I felt more deeply the strong presence and guidance of the Holy Spirit.

The chosen teaching was about the "Spiritual Blessings in Christ" (see Ephesians 1:1-6), which was exactly what I needed to hear at that stage. The preaching delivered raised my faith and hope to a very high level. At the end of the sermon, as people were called to the front to be prayed for, I was already turning the wheels of my chair when the preacher pointed his finger toward me, saying, "Sister, I want to pray for you." Such words were the best ones I could have ever heard to be persuaded of my healing.

FAITH WITHOUT WORKS IS DEAD

Several elders stood around me and prayed. Now was the time for me to demonstrate my faith by my actions. I reminded myself that "Faith without works is dead" (see James 2:26). A lady put her hand on my shoulder and prayed to encourage me to start walking. I was able to advance by shuffling, but unfortunately after a few steps I felt atrocious pains in my spine—worse than ever before. However, although I was in agony in my back, I did not let myself be touched by my feelings. Determined in my actions, I decided not to give up.

❖∾❖∾❖∾❖∾❖∾❖∾❖∾❖∾❖∾❖∾❖

Determined in my actions,
I decided not to give up.

❖∾❖∾❖∾❖∾❖∾❖∾❖∾❖∾❖∾❖∾❖

At the point where I could have stopped myself from trying to walk, at the point where I could have been concerned about the way I was going to appear to people's eyes, I did not let myself be discouraged. Looking to Jesus instead of man, I quickly bent myself, holding the lower part of my spine. I kept advancing; and just as I was doing this, I had a vision of myself walking normally among the people who were in the church. I was living more in the spiritual than in the natural, seeing the unseen as already being seen, as already existing in front of my eyes as it says in the book of Hebrews: "Faith is the substance of things hoped for, the evidence of things not seen" (Hebrews 11:1 NKJV).

When I arrived again in front of my wheelchair, the lady who was walking with me reminded me that—by faith—I had already received my full healing. She also stressed that there was already some manifestation of this healing and that I just had to thank God for it and keep on living by faith and action.

When I looked toward her, she said that it was now time for me to sit down again. Spiritually, at that stage, I had a real connection with God; and instead of sitting down again, I looked at the lady and said, "I want to keep on walking." She looked very surprised and kept on praying beside me, as I continued persevering.

The second time I arrived and stood in front of my wheelchair, that same lady who had been encouraging me all the time said that from now on I was no longer going to need the wheelchair. Obviously I agreed with her. Then, at my greatest surprise, she called my husband, "Mike, come and take the chair and go and put it in the boot of your car." As I watched him pushing the chair out of the church, I was in despair. I really cried out to God. At that point, my body was tired, and I could not take any more steps. I had done all that I could and now, living in the Spirit, I believed that God was going to complete my healing. I reminded myself of the words of Jesus: "I will never leave you nor forsake you."

I did not have the faintest idea of how this was going to happen, but I believed and was convinced that God's power was going to manifest.

THE TURNING POINT LEADING TO VICTORY

As I sat down in the pew with atrocious pains in my spine, a lady from the congregation came to the front and explained how to be relieved of pain in the lower part of the spine. I listened to her as she said, "Stand up, set your feet slightly apart, close your eyes already thanking Jesus for your healing. Then put your hands on your hips and try to turn your body to the right and then to the left. Do not force yourself by turning your body too far. Just do what you can and as you look unto Jesus, gradually your healing will come and you will not have any more pain."

Although I felt unable to perform any physical movement, I got up, set my feet slightly apart, closed my eyes, and confessed my healing by fixing my eyes upon Jesus. I thanked God for His power while I pictured myself turning my body normally to the right and to the left. After a while I suddenly felt something like a bar, like a piece of metal coming off my spine. From then onward my legs became lighter and immediately I was able to walk normally again. At this precise moment, I could also lift up my arms, bend my knees, move my body, and even run!

God had performed a healing miracle!

God had performed a healing miracle, and immediately He received all His glory from everyone in the church. It was such a wonderful feeling for me to have regained my physical abilities that I testified this by calling my relatives in France, telling my friends, the several churches who were praying for me, and then YWAM where I returned the following week as a walking miracle.

I will never forget how surprised my doctor was when I called him the following morning. My relatives-in-law were also astounded when we all met for dinner the following week. After seeing me in a wheelchair at my niece's wedding, they now saw me standing up and walking normally. Glory be to God, our Healer!

*Sunday after my healing with the lady
who had been praying for me.*

WITNESSING AND HEALINGS IN 2001

In the year 2001, my interests increased in witnessing God's healing power and in encouraging those who were sick. I continued to recover from my brain tumor, but the doctors wanted me to have another MRI in February (my fifth since October 1998). I was still involved in my tutoring, in attending healing meetings, studying for a few hours at the Bible college, and driving to YWAM on Friday evenings.

After experiencing God's power over me, and as Ross Tooley writes in his book entitled *You Cannot But Tell*, I could not help myself from witnessing God's goodness in several churches, to my French relatives when I called them, and to those I was praying for at some home fellowships. I still remember how one day, one lady was healed of her frozen shoulder and her husband of his aching right hip. Another day I prayed and laid my hand upon the stomach of one lady who, when she saw her doctor at the hospital the following week, was told that she no longer needed an operation. Glory be to God alone for these healings!

❀∾❀∾❀∾❀∾❀∾❀∾❀∾❀∾❀∾❀∾❀

Glory be to God alone for these healings!

❀∾❀∾❀∾❀∾❀∾❀∾❀∾❀∾❀∾❀∾❀

At the end of 2001, I was looking forward more than ever before to what my future was going to bring me; but, once more, I had to face a new test and fight another good fight of faith.

POINTS TO PONDER

The following verse brought much comfort:

Consider it pure joy, my brothers and sisters, whenever you face trials of many kinds, because you know that the testing of your faith produces perseverance. Let persever-ance finish its work so that you may be mature and com-plete, not lacking anything (James 1:2-4 NIV).

How hard is it for you to "Consider it pure joy" when you are facing physical, emotional, or spiritual trials?

Many people were praying for the author's healing. Do you be-lieve God still performs miracles today?

Although the world is full of suffering, it is also full of the overcoming of it.
—Helen Keller (1880-1968).

Helen Keller was both deaf and blind, but her fierce motivation to show herself she could overcome manifested in enabling her to become the first person with both of these afflictions to graduate from college.

Healing is a matter of time, but it is sometimes also a matter of opportunity.
—Hippocrates (460 BC-370 BC).

It is said that no historical figure did more for medicine than Hippocrates.

4

2002—ANOTHER BATTLE, ANOTHER VICTORY

4

2002—ANOTHER BATTLE, ANOTHER VICTORY

Trust in the Lord with all your heart and lean not on your own understanding; in all your ways acknowledge him, and he will make your paths straight (Proverbs 3:5-6 NIV).

As I was enjoying the benefits of all my recoveries, at the beginning of the year 2002 it was announced on Christian television that a Healing Miracles Crusade would take place in Australia at the Sydney Entertainment Center in June. This gave me the strong desire to go and worship God at that place. I believed that worshiping God among thousands of people was all I would need to be restored of pain in my ribs and to walk normally instead of slowly all the time.

Financially, the number of my weekly teaching lessons had increased and so enabled me to pay for my flight and hotel in Sydney. Everything was very promising, and I was really looking forward to the crusade. Unfortunately, my joy was sapped in April when one morning, as I got up, I was unable to lift up my feet. As I was shuffling and staggering, I had to use a wheelchair again.

I was brokenhearted from this sudden setback. It was the third time since 1999 that I was facing a trial. Physically weak again, I could have let myself be influenced by the words of Job in Job 33:29 (NIV) saying that, "God does all these things to a person—twice, even three times," but instead I preferred to believe that once more God had let satan have my health but was not going to let him have my life. In the very end, satan, who had already been defeated twice, was going to lose another battle. I was going to be the winner, and God was going to be glorified again.

My favorite songs at that time were the ones reminding me to live: "One Day at a Time," and I also focused on how "The Joy of the Lord Is My Strength."

These Scriptures encouraged me all the more:

> He [God] *is a rewarder of those who diligently seek Him* (Hebrews 11:6 NKJV).

> *…God causes everything to work together for the good of those who love God…* (Romans 8:28).

> *Do not grieve, for the joy of the Lord is your strength* (Nehemiah 8:10 NIV).

Concerned about the condition of my brain, the neurosurgeon scheduled me for another MRI (my sixth since 1998). A 1 millimeter (.04 inch) abnormality was detected in the center of my brain. I was disappointed by such a result, but did not lose hope after such news. Many people prayed over me, and a French friend of mine, Michel, from Albany, came to pray over me. After he left my house, as I was sitting in the front room, I found much encouragement in reading Psalm 103:1-3 (NKJV):

Bless the Lord, O my soul; and all that is within me, bless His holy name! Bless the Lord, O my soul, and forget not all His benefits: who forgives all your iniquities, who heals all your diseases.

I kept reading the Bible; and at one point, after asking God where I could find a Scripture about healing in the book of Proverbs, my eyes suddenly fell on Proverbs 3:7-8 (NKJV):

...Fear the Lord and depart from evil. It will bring health to your flesh, and strength to your bones.

Such words really filled me with hope, and after a while I felt my toes becoming hot. As I looked at them, I saw that they were very red. A change was definitely happening. Instead of keeping my feet on the floor, I started trying to move my right foot by very slowly bending its toes. When I became able to bend all of them completely, the sole of my right foot was no longer flat, and I was able to lift up my foot from the floor.

Similarly, I exercised the toes of my left foot, and slowly I was able to bend them too. From the time when I could bend all of them totally, I was able to lift up my left foot completely from the floor. I had regained strength in both feet, which were now functioning normally. As I got up, I saw that I could not only walk but could also raise my arms normally. I had just been touched by God who had made me whole by His healing power over my feet, legs, arms, and whole body.

❀∽❀∽❀∽❀∽❀∽❀∽❀∽❀∽❀∽❀∽❀

*I had just been touched by God
who had made me whole.*

❀∽❀∽❀∽❀∽❀∽❀∽❀∽❀∽❀∽❀∽❀

The first one to see this miracle was my husband. A few hours earlier he had seen me at home in a wheelchair, and now he could see me arriving at his office—after driving the car and walking normally! Satan had been defeated once more and I was now able to realize the desire of my heart which was to go, a few weeks later, to the healing miracle crusade.

During the month of May, I did not overdo it in my daily routine. I also showed wisdom in the way I traveled to Sydney by using a wheelchair to get in and out of the plane. Even so, at the end of the day of my arrival in Sydney, I was in agony in my ribs and back, which I could hardly move. I went to bed early and rested in my hotel room the following morning. A friend of mine came to join me at lunch time, and at 3 o'clock in the afternoon, we went to the entertainment center for the crusade that was going to start a few hours later.

RECEIVING MY HEALING

After the teaching, I felt God touching me during the praise and worship time. My hands suddenly became boiling hot, and I also felt electricity in my arms. Just as I started feeling this, Pastor Benny Hinn announced that some people were, right at that moment, feeling heat in their hands and electricity in their arms, which was the sign of their healing.

Hearing these words was the confirmation of God's healing power upon me, a healing that enabled me to fly back to Perth without using the wheelchair at the airport. Since that date, I have felt no more pain in my ribs.

On the second evening of the crusade, my legs were shaking when people testified their healing on the stage of the auditorium.

Physically, I knew that something was happening in my body, and my faith and hope increased.

One afternoon two weeks later, I was shopping in the Park Shopping Center in Victoria Park, a place where I very rarely shopped. As there was not much time left before closing time, I asked and thanked the Holy Spirit for guiding me in the grocery store. Just as I said, "I love You Jesus," I suddenly felt vibrations all over me and started walking at a normal speed instead of making small steps as I had for many years. God's healing power had touched me again and I was completely restored. Soon afterward when I was at my husband's office, he was amazed to see that I could now walk as fast as he did, even when he was purposely walking quickly.

The following week I went to see my doctor. He was amazed to see how my body had been totally and so quickly restored, only two months after the sudden relapse that I had in April. He was so surprised by such a change that immediately he wrote a medical report (see page 86).

In September 2002, I had another MRI (my seventh since 1998). There was no longer an abnormality in my brain. This result being positive, the neurosurgeon decided, for the first time since 1998, that I did not need a follow-up MRI for another two years.

A BODY RESTORED

As time went on, my health kept improving by an increase in my physical activities. I was now leading a normal life and driving much longer distances without feeling any pain in my ribs. After being in agony for years, nothing could have been more appreciated by me than being able to live without pain. It was such a relief to have my body restored!

❀∽❀∽❀∽❀∽❀∽❀∽❀∽❀∽❀∽❀∽❀∽❀

It was such a relief to have my body restored!

❀∽❀∽❀∽❀∽❀∽❀∽❀∽❀∽❀∽❀∽❀∽❀

Still teaching, I also continued attending Bible classes. My most satisfying enjoyment was to testify and glorify God for His healing power.

In August 2002, I visited our daughter in Melbourne; and in October 2003, I attended a Women's Conference at Christian City church in Oxford Falls, a very remote suburb of Sydney. Then at the beginning of 2004, I booked a flight to Brisbane for another Healing Miracles Crusade with Pastor Benny Hinn at the end of June.

I was really looking forward to experiencing again an amazing time of praise and worship and then witnessing healing miracles when people would rise out of their wheelchairs and walk, and deaf people would suddenly be able to hear. I was really happy about the way my future seemed to be working out.

Unfortunately, my joy of living was sapped again in May 2004 when I had another test, another battle to face. At the time when I was suffering no more sickness in my body, suddenly I had to be prepared for a new time of trials.

POINTS TO PONDER

Bless the Lord, O my soul; and all that is within me, bless His holy name! Bless the Lord, O my soul, and forget not all His benefits: who forgives all your iniquities, who heals all your diseases (Psalm 103:1-3 NKJV).

What does this passage in Psalm 103 mean to you? God's Word, written and spoken, brings comfort and strength—if we take the time to read it and meditate on it with our all our hearts and spirits. Asking the Holy Spirit to help us understand what we read in the Bible is of utmost importance if we want to grow spiritually.

Our days are numbered. One of the primary goals in our lives should be to prepare for our last day. The legacy we leave is not just in our possessions, but in the quality of our lives. What preparations should we be making now? The greatest waste in all of our earth, which cannot be recycled or reclaimed, is our waste of the time that God has given us each day.

–Reverend Billy Graham

5

2004—FALLING AND RISING AGAIN

5

2004—FALLING AND RISING AGAIN

...call upon me in the day of trouble; I will deliver
you, and you will honor me (Psalm 50:15 NIV).

In the morning of Wednesday, May 5, 2004, my body was suddenly affected after I fell heavily on the concrete outside my family room. I hurt myself on the left side of my brain. I felt such a strong pain that I took a bowl with me and went to lie down. Hardly was I in bed a moment when I vomited—a lot. At the same time, my legs started and kept on shaking for quite a while. When they suddenly stopped, I was no longer able to move them at all.

I was facing another attack from satan. How could God have allowed this to happen again and how was He going to rescue me this time?

My husband drove me to see the neurosurgeon who booked me for another MRI of my brain (my eighth since 1998). The result was good. No medical problem was diagnosed.

This time I decided not tell very many people about the relapse.

As I was again dragging my feet and unable to lift up my arms, I was sent under observation at Galliers Hospital in Armadale where my doctor visited me on a regular basis. Every day the nurse helped me shower, change my clothes, and put me in bed. To be spiritually encouraged, I was listening to Scriptures, mainly on healing, and also to songs of worship. My favorite ones were "One Day at a Time" and the song by Parachute Band entitled "Without You." The One I needed most at that time, the only One I really needed was God. I was always touched and many times even burst into tears when I heard the following words in the song:

> I can't live without You.
> I can't walk this road alone.
> In my heart I need You.
> Holy One, come take my hand.

This song helped me to rely more and more on God who was my refuge. I knew that He could help me and deliver me once more; but several times I wished I had been with Him in Heaven rather than on earth without being a good witness of Him.

❖ ∾ ❖ ∾ ❖ ∾ ❖ ∾ ❖ ∾ ❖ ∾ ❖ ∾ ❖ ∾ ❖ ∾ ❖ ∾ ❖

I relied more and more on God
who was my refuge.

❖ ∾ ❖ ∾ ❖ ∾ ❖ ∾ ❖ ∾ ❖ ∾ ❖ ∾ ❖ ∾ ❖ ∾ ❖ ∾ ❖

My situation became difficult to face when, after spending two weeks in the hospital, my doctor announced that according to the medical laws and since I was facing no medical problems, I had to be discharged. He tried to find a respite, rehabilitation facility, but was unsuccessful. On May 27, the only place that would accept me was the Perth Clinic where I arrived late in the morning. I felt discouraged and decided to return home at the end of the same day. From then onward I was spending most of my days by myself at home.

Not being able to bend my knees at all, I had to sleep in a very low bed. To get into it I had to start by putting myself at the very bottom part of the bed. Afterward, I laid my body on the mattress and then pulled myself up to the top of the bed at the level of the pillow on which I could finally rest my head.

My enjoyment continued to be listening to tapes of praise and worship. I also watched television programs and read the Bible during the day. Physically, shuffling made me weak; but spiritually, strength and hope invaded me—especially on the day I read again in the book of James:

> Consider it pure joy, my brothers, whenever you face trials of many kinds, because you know that the testing of your faith develops perseverance. Perseverance must finish its work so that you may be mature and complete, not lacking anything (James 1:2-4 NIV 1984).

Although I was falling in my physical life, I started confessing that I would arise, that in times of darkness God would always be my Light (see Micah 7:8), and that He would never abandon me as it is written in Hebrews 13:5 (NIV): Never will I leave you; never will I forsake you.

A TURNING POINT

On the second day I was home, the fulfillment of the Scriptures came to pass. Saturday, May 29, 2004, was a turning point in my life. My faith and actions were tested again; and again they were turned into a victory.

❀◌❀◌❀◌❀◌❀◌❀◌❀◌❀◌❀◌❀◌❀

My faith and actions were tested again;
and again they were turned into a victory.

❀◌❀◌❀◌❀◌❀◌❀◌❀◌❀◌❀◌❀◌❀

This is how it happened:

A friend of mine, Pat, visited me in the afternoon. She encouraged me for a few hours. She did all she could to increase my hope and, before departing, she prayed over me. At that time as I opened my lips and tried to stretch them to give her a smile, I suddenly felt them shaking and from then on I could no longer use my lips.

Later that evening I did not have the desire to read my Bible. However, I had a guilty conscience for the way I was acting; so I decided to read a commentary about the book of Romans. As I opened the book, my eyes fell on the following lines:

> *We rejoice in the hope of the glory of God. Not only so, but we also rejoice in our sufferings, because we know that suffering produces perseverance; perseverance, character; and character, hope. And hope does not disappoint us* (Romans 5:2-5 NIV 1984).

These words deeply touched me. I suddenly felt the presence of God invading me, and I drew closer to Him. By reading the word "hope," I turned my eyes upon Jesus imagining how beautiful it would be to be face to face with Him in Heaven, a place with no more pain, no more sickness—only smiles. This vision encouraged me so much that instantly I did what I was seeing in the spiritual and instantly I was able to smile, able to use my lips normally again.

FULL OF JOY

Full of joy, I kept smiling, thanking God for His goodness. My faith increased so much that I was now expecting the full healing of my body. Believing that my legs were going to function normally again, I slid them across the bed and put my feet on the floor. For the first time after several weeks I was now able not only to lift up my feet normally but also walk at a normal speed and even take big steps.

The first witness of this healing was my husband. After spending two weeks in the hospital and a few nights at home—alone in a low bed—I was so happy to be able to move my legs again that I quickly changed bedrooms and went to lie down close to my husband in the bed we had shared since 1975. On that unforgettable night, I was thrilled with what God had performed, thanking Him once more for coming to my rescue—being my Healer again.

SHARING GOD'S MIRACLE

After such an experience, my main desire was to testify and glorify God. So three days later I drove to see the doctor in charge of the Perth Clinic where I had spent the afternoon of May 27. As soon as the doctor saw me in the waiting-room, he was amazed, really surprised at my recovery. He asked me several times about my wheel-chair. Then, for the full length of a visit, he asked me many questions about my faith in God, my way of praying, and how the miracle happened. What a wonderful experience it was to share God's goodness and see a doctor so eager to know about Christianity.

The following week, I drove to my doctor's medical center. He was also amazed. Medically speaking, as he wrote in his report, there was no explanation.

The following are two reports written by the reputable medical doctor, Dr. Ivor Francis Desouza.[1] I give God all the glory for what the reports testify about the miracle I received.

PROGRESS NOTES
As at 11th July 2002.

Patient Details:

Patient Name: Ms Claudine Bray
Address:

Phone - Home:
Phone - Work:
D.O.B.:
Record Number:
Medicare Number:

Allergies:

Progress Notes:

Thursday July 11 2002   15:09:05
Dr. I.F. De Souza

My patient Claudine Bray went to a healing miracle crusade in Sydney on the 7-8 June 2002 organized by pastor Benny Hinn, and had a remarkable improvement in her paralysis of the leg from a brain tumour in the temporal lobe.
Her clinical signs of the left lower limbs and her very bad limp has altogether gone. She can now walk normally and even exercise and run normally

Yours sincerely,

Dr I F Desouza.
BSc(Hons).,MBBS., DRACOG., FRACGP.   MFM, MGP Psyche, Grad Dip Med .

8th June 2004

Dr. I.F. De Souza
B.Sc(Hons) MBBS DRACOG Dip FM MFM Grad Dip GP Psyc

To whom it may concern

Re: **Claudine Bray**

This is to certify that I had examined Claudine Bray on the 9th May 2004 at Armadale Hospital and found her unable to walk due to hyporeflexia associated with collapse and tremor. She was seen by a physician, a neurologist and a psychiatrist, all of whom were unable to help manage her.

I saw Mrs Bray again on 8th June 2004 and found that she was walking normally without weakness or paralysis. She also saw a Psychiatrist, who also could not believe the improvement in her symptoms. I have no explanation of the improvement in her symptoms

Yours faithfully

DR I F DESOUZA

Satan had put me under trials in May 2004—but once more he was defeated. He had tried to prevent me from attending a Healing Miracles Crusade, but instead of winning, he became the loser; he was the victim of his actions, and I was the victor, able to witness about God and His healing power and to thank Him as it is written:

Give thanks to the Lord and proclaim his greatness. Let the whole world know what he has done. Sing to him; yes, sing his praises. Tell everyone about his wonderful deeds (Psalm 105:1-2).

At the June crusade in Brisbane, it was announced that a tour to Israel would be organized for the month of November. Many people desiring to go there were prayed for to receive all the financial provisions they would need. I was part of that group, and not long after my return to Perth, I was amazed by the increase I had in my number of students. I still thank God for the way He provided me the finances I needed.

He provided me the finances I needed.

Not very long before the tour to the Holy Land, at the end of October, I clearly heard a very small voice saying, "Send your testimony on the Internet to the Benny Hinn Ministries." I was really surprised to hear such words and also very perplexed by hearing them so suddenly and so unexpectedly. I had already tried to write all my experiences, but had never succeeded to summarize them in 1,000 characters—including commas, periods, and spaces—which the Website required of those submitting testimonies.

I really could not imagine how I would be able to do it this time, but I obeyed the voice I had just heard. Straightaway I sat at my desk, asked the Holy Spirit to guide me, and then started typing the following document with the hope of telling the world of God's mercy and faithfulness. (I will let you know later on what was the result of this article.)

Taking the Saving, Healing Power of Jesus Christ to the World

Miracle Follow-Up

Home
Prayer
Events
Broadcast
Partners
Shopping
Missions
Donate
Resources
About BHM
En Español

Testimony Form

Please enter your testimony information below.
Press the Submit button after you are finished.
* = Required Items

If your testimony is physical in nature, would you be able to provide
medical documentation? ⦿ Yes ○ No

First Name: CLAUDINE *
Last Name: BRAY *
Address 1: *
Address 2:
City: *
State: U.S. Only
Zip/Postal Code: *
Country: Australia *
Home Phone: *
Work Phone:
Other Phone:
Email Address: claudine@tribal.net.au *

Briefly State Your Testimony: * (1000 character limit) 4 characters avail.

In Nov 1998. Diagnosis of brain tumour and paralysis
in legs during the night. In wheel-chair attended
church to be anointed with oil.Spent 6 weeks at Hosp
Physically- in agony and lost 8 kilos(a nurse called
the pastor after my first night at hospital Several
visions.Heard God saying 'Without faith it is impos
sible to please God'. In Dec slid myself out of bed,
made few steps pushing chair and gradually became
able to walk again. Back home, improved. However re
lapsed in June 1999.Had craniotomy operation. Then
Feb 2000 disc herniation of the spine.Wheel-chair,5
weeks,then miraculously healed in church. Was watch
ing THIS IS YOUR DAY on TV and planned HMC Sydney in
June 2002.Unfortuntely had a relapse,new MRI andwas
weak in Apr. However could still attend crusade.
Frid evening during praise and worship, hot hands
and electricity in my arms: full healing of pains in
ribs and spine. Sat evening very shaky legs. Two
weeks later walked, ran and exercised. Soon I will be
in Jerusalem!

THE HOLY LAND TOUR

During my visit to Israel, I felt a very special atmosphere and I
found that this country, although small in size, is very powerful in
the way it can touch its visitors. Many times in the past I had heard

several church ministers say that Christians would definitely feel the presence of Jesus on the day they visit His homeland. I had this experience in the Dead Sea and even more in the Garden of Gethsemane, the place where Jesus last walked on earth before dying for us on the Cross.

My trip to the Holy Land wonderfully ended the year 2004 and was followed a few months later by an amazing way of glorifying God and encouraging many people in all the nations.

At the Dead Sea, we were told that putting mud where healing was desired confirmed our faith.

The Garden of Gethsemane where Jesus prayed.

MY TESTIMONY OF GOD'S MIRACLE

As already mentioned, a voice told me to submit my testimony of all my healings to the Benny Hinn Ministries. To my greatest surprise, I typed all the information needed between 1998 and 2004. Then after pressing "Submit", I said to the Holy Spirit that I had obeyed Him and that from now on everything was in His hands—my desire was to reach all the nations testifying the goodness of God to the whole world. The reason I had clearly heard the Holy Spirit asking me to write to the Benny Hinn Ministries was revealed to me in January 2005 when I received the fulfilment of the words written in the book of Hebrews:

And it is impossible to please God without faith. Anyone who wants to come to him must believe that God exists and that he rewards those who sincerely seek him (Hebrews 11:6)

ENDNOTE

1. Dr. Desouza's earned credentials include: Bachelor of Science with Honors; Bachelor of Medicine/Bachelor of Surgery; Diploma of Royal Australian College of Obstetricians and Gynaecologists; Fellow of the Royal Australian College of General Practitioners; Master of Forensic Medicine; Master of General Practice Psychiatry; Graduate Diploma in Medicine (Specializing in Pain Management).

POINTS TO PONDER

Discouragement comes quickly to those who have no faith in God and His everlasting grace and mercy. Facing several physical setbacks, the author kept her spiritual well-being lifted high and holy by acknowledging His healings and never blaming Him. Does her attitude and strength empower you to tackle whatever may come your way? What Scriptures do you find especially comforting and encouraging?

> *"For I know the plans I have for you," says the Lord. "They are plans for good and not for disaster, to give you a future and a hope"* (Jeremiah 29:11).

> Believers, look up—take courage. The angels are nearer than you think.
>
> —Reverend Billy Graham

> Many people ruin their health and their lives by taking the poison of bitterness, resentment and unforgiveness. Matthew 18:23-35 tells us that if we do not forgive people, we get turned over to the torturers.
>
> —Joyce Meyer

6

2005—OBEDIENCE BRINGS REWARDS

6

2005—OBEDIENCE BRINGS REWARDS

If you fully obey the Lord your God and carefully keep all his commands that I am giving you today, the Lord your God will set you high above all the nations of the world (Deuteronomy 28:1).

I certainly would have never imagined that my experiences would one day be used to glorify God and be a blessing to others in all the nations. In 1998 I had faced the most difficult and painful year in my life, very suddenly affected by a brain tumor, in real darkness for many months. Seven years later, in 2005, I was surprised by the way the year started. Instead of being in the dark, I was now a light of God's power as it is written in the book of Isaiah:

Arise…Let your light shine for all to see. For the glory of the Lord rises to shine on you (Isaiah 60:1).

On very early morning in January 2005, I was suddenly awakened by the sound of the phone. As soon as I picked it up, I heard a lady's voice say, "This is the Benny Hinn Ministries from America. The report you sent to us on the Internet has been chosen to be published in our monthly magazine, *Your Day*, in the month of August. We are sending you a form which will have to be completed by two doctors and returned to us as soon as possible."

What a joy, what a surprise it was for me to have been selected.

Receiving in Australia such news from the United States—the other side of the world—shows that God is not and will never be limited by the distance. This phone call from America brought back to my memory how, a few months before, I had heard the soft voice of the Holy Spirit asking me to send my healing testimonies to the Benny Hinn Ministries. Although I had not understood the reason why I had been requested to do this so suddenly, I had obeyed straightaway. I believe that my obedience enabled me to fulfill my desire of glorifying God and also encouraging people in many countries.

*Obedience, hope, and faith expressed by
our actions are what we need to be blessed.*

Obedience, hope, and faith expressed by our actions are what we all need to put into practice to be blessed and then be a blessing to others and also bring glory to God for His power and goodness toward all of us.

I attended seven Benny Hinn conferences between 2002 and 2009, Sydney (twice), Brisbane, Auckland (twice), Paris, and Christchurch. The following is the article published in the Benny Hinn Ministries magazine.

• Jesus, You promised, *"And this gospel of the kingdom shall be preached in all the world for a witness unto all nations; and then shall the end come"* (Matthew 24:14).

As you read and study the Scriptures, the *logos* (written Word) will become *rhema* (living revelation Word) in your life. Psalm 80:18 declares, *"Quicken us, and we will call upon thy name."* The Word arouses and activates His power in you. And once the quickening comes, you will pray and intercede with greater power.

Praying in the Name of Jesus

The name of Jesus has given you the authority to be victorious in prayer! The Bible declares that *anything* we ask will be accomplished when we pray in Jesus's name. These powerful promises come from the lips of the Master Himself:

> *Whatsoever ye shall ask the Father in my name, he will give it you.* (John 16:23)

> *If ye shall ask any thing in my name, I will do it.* (John 14:14)

> *If two of you shall agree on earth as touching any thing that they shall ask, it shall be done for them of my Father which is in heaven. For where two or three are gathered together in my name, there am I in the midst of them.* (Matthew 18:19-20)

As believers we have been given unlimited use of Jesus's name. When we pray in Jesus's name, we go in His authority and in His place, professing the power of His awesome, mighty name.

Pray in faith and confidence. Jesus said, *"Verily, verily, I say unto you, Whatsoever ye shall ask the Father in my name, he will give it you. Hitherto have ye asked nothing in my name: ask, and ye shall receive, that your joy may be full"* (John 16:23-24). "Verily, verily" means, "I vow, I vow." Jesus said, "I guarantee it; I give you My word. Whatever you ask of the Father in My name, He will give it to you!"

Intercessory prayer is a powerful weapon available to God's children for use against the enemy. Persistent intercessory prayer produces results and unleashes supernatural power for victory. In the words of E. M. Bounds, "Our praying needs to be pressed and pursued with an energy that never tires, a persistency which will not be denied, and a courage which never fails."

Omnipotent and mighty, intercessory prayer is a force that crosses the borders of time and invites the eternal power of God into your life and into the lives of your loved ones!

CANADA: P.O. Box 638, Station U • Toronto, Ontario M8Z 5Y9; **EUROPE:** P.O. Box 30319 • London NW10 7ZP • England; **AUSTRALIA:** P.O. Box 2422 • Mansfield, QLD 4122; **NEW ZEALAND:** P.O. Box 54206 • Wellington; **INDIA:** P.O. Box 5505 • Bangalore GPO 560 001 • Karnataka; **PHILIPPINES:** P.O. Box 4475, Manila Central Post Office • 1084 Manila; **AFRICA:** Private Bag X54335 • Durban, South Africa; **HONG KONG:** GPO Box 1600 • Hong Kong; **JAPAN:** P.O. Box 35 • Nakamura Post Office 453-8799 • Nagoya, Japan; **USA/ALL OTHERS:** P.O. Box 162000 • Irving, Texas 75016-2000 • USA ©2005 World Healing Center Church • P.O. Box 16200 Irving, Texas 75016-2000 • www.BennyHinn.org

Miracle Stream

November 1998 was a horrible month. Australian Claudine Bray was diagnosed and hospitalized with a brain tumor.

"I was unable to walk due to a sudden onset of paralysis in my legs," she remembers. I went through weeks of hospitalization. It was the first of several trials to come."

In June 1999, surgery was performed to remove a six-inch cancerous piece of tissue from her brain. After six months of recovery, she again lost the ability to use her legs and feet and became confined to a wheelchair. Over the next several months she spent much of her time lying in bed watching television. *This Is Your Day!* with Pastor Benny was a great encouragement through the tragedies and depression she experienced. Then in 2002, she heard about an upcoming Benny Hinn Miracle Crusade scheduled for Sydney, Australia.

"During the services," Claudine recalls, "I felt the heat of God's power. The pain left. My legs began to shake uncontrollably. I knew something happened, but it was two weeks before the healing actually happened. I was shopping in a grocery store and began to feel the presence of God. As I began to praise Jesus and tell Him how much I loved Him, I felt vibrations go through my body. I got out of the wheelchair and began walking and eventually running. The doctor's report even mentions the Benny Hinn crusade!"

Claudine Bray

A terrible fall two years later seemed to set her back, but by this time she had learned to walk in victory. As her faith surged through the reading of God's Word, the physicians were amazed once again, and today she leads a healthy life.

"These experiences have given me a keen awareness of the sufferings of others," Claudine shares. "I know what it means to go through the valley of despair. And I know what God can do when you call out to Him. I definitely believe in His ability to heal!"

Article published in the Benny Hinn Ministries magazine.

MORE GOOD NEWS

Although I had totally recovered and was able to lead a normal life, medically speaking the conditions of my brain had to be followed up. After seven years of tests, I was really fed up with having to go through the same process again. However, good news was on the way. After my ninth MRI since 1998, the neurosurgeon announced that I would be given a gap of four years before I had to have another MRI.

Such a statement was a real relief for me and a good way to increase my faith and hope for total restoration recognized by the medical team.

POINTS TO PONDER

"Obedience, hope, and faith expressed by our actions are what we all need to put into practice to be blessed and then be a blessing to others and also bring glory to God for His power and goodness toward all of us." This is a powerful statement filled with truth and confidence. These are the qualities Christians need to express through actions to receive blessings and to give blessings to others—most of all we must bring glory to God for He is the source of all that is good and right. How are you at obeying, being hopeful, and having faith?

> If we cannot believe God when circumstances seem to be against us, we do not believe Him at all.
>
> –Charles Spurgeon

> Christian, remember the goodness of God in the frost of adversity.
>
> –Charles Spurgeon

> Trials teach us what we are; they dig up the soil, and let us see what we are made of.
>
> –Charles Spurgeon

7

2008-2009—SUDDEN SORROW, BUT GOD GLORIFIED

7

2008-2009—SUDDEN SORROW, BUT GOD GLORIFIED

I am still confident of this: I will see the goodness of the Lord in the land of the living (Psalm 27:13 NIV).

MY MOST FRIGHTENING NIGHT

In the book of Job it says that God gives and God takes away.

In April 2008, our family was given a wonderful miracle—a granddaughter, Chloe. My husband and I went to welcome her into the world in Melbourne in May. While we were there, I attended church in the suburb of Knox where it was announced that a ladies conference would take place the last weekend in August. The topic was already named "Joy," and I was so attracted by such a title that I decided to register. What a wonderful plan for the month of August—seeing my granddaughter again and finding out how to experience more joy in life.

A few months later, on July 5, my husband and I celebrated our 33rd wedding anniversary. The following month, for no special reason, Mike and I decided to spend another special night in a hotel on August 9, 2008. On that day, we relaxed in the afternoon in our hotel room before attending church and enjoying dinner at the restaurant. We shared good conversation and, although it was cold, when we walked out of the restaurant, my husband walked as if we were having a leisurely stroll. I was so amazed by what was happening to both of us during the whole evening that before we switched the light off, I even said to God, "I am really amazed, God, to see how we are becoming closer to one another tonight."

I was really looking forward to what was going to happen to us as a couple in the future—a bright and beautiful future indeed.

Then, that same evening, my husband who was very fit, never sick, swam regularly, played golf, and rode his bike every day—suffered a massive heart attack, which started at the hotel and finished at the hospital at 3:15 A.M. I clearly remember hearing the voice of one doctor saying, "He is dead."

What I had never imagined came to pass. I was brokenhearted, disappointed, lonely, and very confused. My life had suddenly changed—in a way I could not comprehend the situation I was facing. Attending the funeral was such a painful experience that I had totally rejected the thought of being part of the ladies conference in Melbourne at the end of August. However, my daughters and a few friends encouraged me to fulfill what had been my desire. The words they spoke to me were, "You should still go and listen to the preaching about joy. Although you don't feel like doing this now, God might have something special for you at that conference. Just go." What a blessing it was to listen to their advice. Instead of letting myself be totally controlled by my emotions, I was filled with encouragement for facing widowhood and looking into my future with hope.

I was amazed at what happened at the conference. The first meeting started with praise and worship, which was followed by words from the pastor of the church who asked the musicians to play again the song "Amazing Grace"—it was good to hear this song again, but also very painful as it reminded me of my husband's funeral two weeks before. Then, after welcoming everyone, the pastor announced that she had recently seen her mother dying at the hospital, which was another similarity to my own experience. At the closing of the first evening's services, those who had lost a relative were invited to come to the front of the auditorium to be prayed for. I was really touched when I heard the lady pastor say, "I feel this happened to some of you very recently." I was encouraged by other parts of the conference, especially the session related to how to face the loss of someone.

By attending this conference two weeks after my husband died, I learned that when we plan to do something, we should always follow through—even if our circumstances have changed, even if emotionally we no longer feel like doing it. Even when we feel abandoned, God is still with us, encouraging us through the words of other people facing the same experience as ours.

My whole time of grieving was still very hard to go through. However, as time passed, my way of looking at life slowly changed. Although it had been very painful to see my husband starting to die at the hotel, I realized, said, and then truly accepted that his sudden death had been the best for him, for me, and also for my family. A nurse had said to me, "He is very sick, and if we can keep him alive, he will be here for a long time."

The words that encouraged me the most at the beginning of my widowhood are written in Psalm 71:20 (NIV):

Though you have made me see troubles, many and bitter, you will restore my life again: from the depth of the earth you will again bring me up.

Not only was I very encouraged by this Scripture, but I became more and more hopeful to be totally restored. I accepted widowhood as being the beginning of what God had planned as a good future for me. I started honoring Him for all that had happened in my life.

Instead of worrying about your problems, dear reader, start finding joy in living. I encourage you to read the Bible and keep confessing the words of Psalm 50:15. Hear God saying to you:

And call upon Me in the day of trouble; I will deliver you and you shall honor Me and glorify Me (Amplified Bible).

Be also encouraged by the words written in First Peter 1:6-7:

In this you greatly rejoice, though now for a little while, if need be, you have been grieved by various trials, that the genuineness of your faith, being much more precious than gold that perishes, though it is tested by fire, may be found to praise, honor, and glory at the revelation of Jesus Christ (NKJV).

Express your hope of total recovery. See your weakness turning into strength. Show the joy of bringing praise and glory to God who not only will turn your darkness into light but will also give you hope for all the healings you need—whether for your health, finances, family relations, employment, whatever you are facing.

Do not let yourself be emotionally distraught and disappointed. Instead, I will say it again, turn your eyes upon Jesus, trust Him and "Give all your worries and cares to God, for he cares about you" (1 Peter 5:7).

HIS HEALING POWER

I could totally glorify God for His healing power upon me one year after my husband passed away. This is how it happened: Although I had already had nine MRIs of my brain since 1998, I was scheduled for my tenth one in May 2009. For the first time, I heard the best report from the neurosurgeon, "You do not need to come and see me again. You do not need to have any more MRIs."

I hope, dear reader, that you are now very encouraged by the way God touched me and can touch you. Wait patiently until the victory comes. Remember that satan is the victim and God the victor. Become victorious by always glorifying God for His goodness and power.

Rather than sitting back thinking you have no control, take these actions:

- Push satan out of your life.

- Always hope.

- Trust God.

- Ask Him for what you need.

- Compare yourself to the slow but steady frog that will one day reach the winning line.

- Be determined to be successful and you will.

I like to explain these actions this way:

PUSH satan – Pray and Praise Until Something Happens

HOPE – Have Only Positive Expectations

TRUST – Truly and Totally Rely Upon Spiritual Teaching

ASK – Ask and you will receive.
    Seek and you will find
    Knock and the door will be opened

Be like a FROG   Fully Relying On God

WIN – Worship and Witness God.
    Impress and Impact
    Nations

As Prime Minister Winston Churchill said, "NEVER, NEVER, NEVER GIVE UP!"

Before closing, please say aloud and with all your heart the following words: "Heavenly Father, I believe that Jesus is the Son of God, that He died for us, rose again, and is still alive. I thank You, Lord, right now for forgiving me of my sins and for giving me eternal life."

POINTS TO PONDER

Just when the author thought that her life would be sweet, coupled with her husband, he suffered a fatal, massive heart attack. Her faith was so strong that she survived the heartache and has gone on to thrive—never failing to share God's love and faithfulness. For centuries God has been the Source of hope and healing for millions of people. Is He your hope for healing?

> Fight the good fight of faith, and God will give you spiritual mercies.
>
> —George Whitefield

> When a train goes through a tunnel and it gets dark, you don't throw away the ticket and jump off. You sit still and trust the engineer.
>
> —Corrie ten Boom

> True faith rests upon the character of God and asks no further proof than the moral perfections of the One who cannot lie. It is enough that God has said it.
>
> —A.W. Tozer

CONCLUSION

May he give you the desire of your heart and make all your plans succeed (Psalm 20:4 NIV).

I pray that my experiences have in many ways brought illumination to your life and the insights I have shared will remain in your spirit as you face joys and trials, healings and sufferings. The truths that became apparent to me during the ups and downs of my physical ailments were welcomed and appreciated by a body, soul, and spirit that cried out for answers from the one true Physician—God Almighty.

As easy as it would have been to give up and accept the diagnoses and the naysayers, that still small voice within me was all the encouragement I needed to keep up the good fight of faith in Him, He who never forsakes those who love Him. Year after year something more serious knocked at my door—but year after year I became stronger and stronger in faith and hope.

From initially realizing that nothing is impossible with God to experiencing His love beyond measure and peace that passes all human understanding, my blessed assurance rests permanently and completely on my Lord and Savior. I hope and pray that you never experience weeks of lying in a hospital bed or being wheeled into the operating room for surgery on your brain; I hope and pray that you do not have to go through years of physical pain or that your supportive and loving spouse isn't shockingly taken from you. But even in the midst of whatever life shoves at you, always know that your ever-faithful God is right beside you to comfort you. Nothing this world can do to you can jeopardize the love, mercy, and grace He has in His heart especially for you.

The human body is a wondrous creation of God. From the baby soft skin of a newborn, various shades of eye color and hair, and uniquely shaped noses and toes, to the myriad of heights and weights and intelligence, only the Creator of all there is and will ever be could imagine scratched skin that heals itself, eyes that see naturally and spiritually, noses that smell the essence of the Divine, and toes that walk toward eternity. As (overly) concerned as we are about our height, weight, and IQ—all He sees when He looks at us is beauty through the redemptive act of Jesus, our Savior.

I have shared my *Hope and Healings* with you to be an encouragement and a boost of energy to keep going—to keep on keeping on! If you follow that still small voice that whispers softly to you in the middle of the night or during prayer time or even while driving the car, you will be nudged in the right direction to see your destiny fulfilled. Only God knows the end from the beginning; leaning on His leading will keep you on the right path.

Recently I was researching the biblical meanings of numbers and I was amazed at how many related to my life experiences. I am now going to share a few with you hoping that you too will find connections in some spiritually personal way:

- NUMBER 7 means "To be complete or full." In August 2005, seven years after becoming sick with a brain tumor, I glorified God for His healing power by having an article written in the monthly magazine *Your Day* published by Benny Hinn Ministries.

- NUMBER 14 means "Double measure of perfection." The year 2012 was fourteen years after 1998 when I became sick. In this fourteenth year, the following double measures took place:

  ❖ In March 2012 I heard a soft voice saying to me, "Go back to your book." I had tried to write a book previously; but not knowing how the book could be published, I stopped writing and did not think anymore about it. Suddenly my desire to write my own story was revived after hearing God's voice.

  ❖ In May 2012 I had already started rewriting my book when I was prophesied over by Pastor Amanda Wells who said, "It's a new season. Release creative ideas, release creative ideas."

  ❖ In June 2012 I received an email from a publisher who had been contacted by Amanda and who was interested in my book.

- NUMBER 15 means "Divine perfection." In 2013, fifteen years after being very sick in 1998, I will be glorifying God when this book, *Hope and Healings*, will be published by a worldwide publisher of Christian books—who contacted me himself in June 2012!

Hear God's voice, obey Him, and you will discover the amazing plan He has for your future, the desire you always hoped for but never thought would be fulfilled. Because the divinely inspired Scriptures say so much more than I or any other person can ever say, I offer a few verses in this conclusion that confirm our great and mighty God's faithfulness to His children—you and me.

> *"For I know the plans I have for you," says the Lord. "They are plans for good and not for disaster, **to give you a future and a hope"** (Jeremiah 29:11).*

> *And we believers also groan, even though we have the Holy Spirit within us as a foretaste of **future glory**, for we long for our bodies to be released from sin and suffering. We, too, wait with eager **hope** for the day when God will give us our full rights as his adopted children, including the new bodies he has promised us (Romans 8:23).*

> *Make every effort to keep yourselves united in the Spirit, binding yourselves together with peace. For there is one body and one Spirit, just as you have been called to one **glorious hope for the future**. There is one Lord, one faith, one baptism, and one God and Father, who is over all and in all and living through all (Ephesians 4:3-6).*

I leave you with the same admonition that I wrote in the Preface, "Don't let yourself become discouraged; instead, see yourself already as a winner—as a victor and not a victim, one who will become stronger than ever before. The harder your test, the more empowered you will become."

I hope you have enjoyed reading this book, and I sincerely hope that you will adopt a new outlook on life—one of success and strength, hope and healing.

*In 1975
before I was married.*

Today, 2013

GOD'S WORD ON HOPE AND HEALING

Scriptures Verses on Healing

The following Scriptures are short enough to be memorized—or written on a card and carried with you for easy reference. Having these words from God in your heart and mind will bring you hope and healing day and night.

Exodus 15:26 NKJV – If you diligently heed the voice of the LORD your God and do what is right in His sight, give ear to His commandments and keep all His statutes, I will put none of the diseases on you which I have brought on the Egyptians. For I am the LORD who heals you.

Deuteronomy 32:39 NKJV – Now see that I, even I, am He, And there is no God besides Me; I kill and I make alive; I wound and I heal; nor is there any who can deliver from My hand.

2 Chronicles 7:14 NKJV – If My people who are called by My name will humble themselves, and pray and seek My

face, and turn from their wicked ways, then I will hear from heaven, and will forgive their sin and heal their land.

Psalm 30:2 NKJV – O LORD my God, I cried out to You, and You healed me.

Psalm 6:2 NKJV – Have mercy on me, O LORD, for I am weak; O LORD, heal me, for my bones are troubled.

Psalm 103:1-4 NKJV – Bless the LORD, O my soul; and all that is within me, bless His holy name! Bless the LORD, O my soul, and forget not all His benefits: who forgives all your iniquities, who heals all your diseases, who redeems your life from destruction, who crowns you with lovingkindness and tender mercies.

Psalm 107:20 NKJV – He sent His word and healed them, and delivered them from their destructions.

Psalm 147:3 NKJV – He heals the brokenhearted and binds up their wounds.

Proverbs 3:7-8 NKJV – Do not be wise in your own eyes; fear the LORD and depart from evil. It will be health to your flesh, and strength to your bones.

Proverbs 4:20-22 NKJV – My son, give attention to my words; incline your ear to my sayings. Do not let them depart from your eyes; Keep them in the midst of your heart; for they are life to those who find them, and health to all their flesh.

Isaiah 53:5 NKJV – But He was wounded for our transgressions, He was bruised for our iniquities; the chastisement for our peace was upon Him, and by His stripes we are healed.

Isaiah 58:8 NKJV – Then your light shall break forth like the morning, your healing shall spring forth speedily, and your righteousness shall go before you; the glory of the LORD shall be your rear guard.

Isaiah 61:1 NKJV – The Spirit of the Lord GOD is upon Me, because the LORD has anointed Me to preach good tidings to the poor; He has sent Me to heal the broken-hearted, to proclaim liberty to the captives, and the opening of the prison to those who are bound.

Jeremiah 3:22 NKJV – "Return, you backsliding children, and I will heal your backslidings." "Indeed we do come to You, for You are the LORD our God."

Jeremiah 17:14 NKJV – Heal me, O LORD, and I shall be healed; save me, and I shall be saved, for You are my praise.

Jeremiah 30:17 NKJV – For I will restore health to you and heal you of your wounds, says the LORD, because they called you an outcast saying: "This is Zion; no one seeks her."

Jeremiah 33:6 NKJV – Behold, I will bring it health and healing; I will heal them and reveal to them the abundance of peace and truth.

Hosea 6:1 NKJV – Come, and let us return to the LORD; for He has torn, but He will heal us; He has stricken, but He will bind us up.

Hosea 14:4 NKJV – I will heal their backsliding, I will love them freely, for My anger has turned away from him.

Malachi 4:2 NKJV – But to you who fear My name The Sun of Righteousness shall arise with healing in His wings; and you shall go out and grow fat like stall-fed calves.

Matthew 4:23 NKJV – And Jesus went about all Galilee, teaching in their synagogues, preaching the gospel of the kingdom, and healing all kinds of sickness and all kinds of disease among the people.

Matthew 8:13 NKJV – Then Jesus said to the centurion, "Go your way; and as you have believed, so let it be done for you." And his servant was healed that same hour.

Matthew 8:16 NKJV – When evening had come, they brought to Him many who were demon-possessed. And He cast out the spirits with a word, and healed all who were sick.

Matthew 9:35 NKJV – Then Jesus went about all the cities and villages, teaching in their synagogues, preaching the gospel of the kingdom, and healing every sickness and every disease among the people.

Matthew 10:1 NKJV – And when He had called His twelve disciples to Him, He gave them power over unclean spirits, to cast them out, and to heal all kinds of sickness and all kinds of disease.

Matthew 10:8 NKJV – Heal the sick, cleanse the lepers, raise the dead, cast out demons. Freely you have received, freely give.

Matthew 12:22 NKJV – Then one was brought to Him who was demon-possessed, blind and mute; and He healed him, so that the blind and mute man both spoke and saw.

Matthew 14:14 NKJV – And when Jesus went out He saw a great multitude; and He was moved with compassion for them, and healed their sick.

Luke 6:19 NKJV – And the whole multitude sought to touch Him, for power went out from Him and healed them all.

Luke 9:6 NKJV – So they departed and went through the towns, preaching the gospel and healing everywhere. (The twelve are sent out.)

Luke 10:8-9 NKJV – Whatever city you enter, and they receive you, eat such things as are set before you. And heal the sick there, and say to them, "The kingdom of God has come near to you."

Luke 17:15 NKJV – And one of them, when he saw that he was healed, returned, and with a loud voice glorified God. (The story of the ten lepers.)

Acts 3:12 NKJV – So when Peter saw it, he responded to the people: "Men of Israel, why do you marvel at this? Or why look so intently at us, as though by our own power or godliness we had made this man walk?"

Acts 4:29-31 NKJV (Healing of the lame man at the Gate Beautiful) – "Now, Lord, look on their threats, and grant to Your servants that with all boldness they may speak Your word, by stretching out Your hand to heal, and that signs and wonders may be done through the name of Your holy Servant Jesus." And when they had prayed, the place where they were assembled together was shaken; and they were all filled with the Holy Spirit, and they spoke the word of God with boldness.

1 Corinthians 12:9 NKJV – to another faith by the same Spirit, to another gifts of healings by the same Spirit.

James 5:14-16 NKJV – Is anyone among you sick? Let him call for the elders of the church, and let them pray over him, anointing him with oil in the name of the Lord. And the prayer of faith will save the sick, and the Lord will raise him up. And if he has committed sins, he will be forgiven. Confess your trespasses to one another, and pray for one another, that you may be healed. The effective, fervent prayer of a righteous man avails much.

Revelation 22:2 NKJV – In the middle of its street, and on either side of the river, was the tree of life, which bore twelve fruits, each tree yielding its fruit every month. The leaves of the tree were for the healing of the nations.

Luke 8:47 NKJV – Now when the woman saw that she was not hidden, she came trembling; and falling down before Him, she declared to Him in the presence of all the people the reason she had touched Him and how she was healed immediately.

Luke 8:48 NKJV – And He said to her, "Daughter, be of good cheer; your faith has made you well. Go in peace."

Luke 5:17 NKJV – Now it happened on a certain day, as He was teaching, that there were Pharisees and teachers of the law sitting by, who had come out of every town of Galilee, Judea, and Jerusalem. And the power of the Lord was present to heal them.

HOPE-FILLED SCRIPTURES

Psalm 146:5 NIV – Blessed are those whose help is the God of Jacob, whose hope is in the LORD their God.

Psalm 147:11 NIV – the LORD delights in those who fear him, who put their hope in his unfailing love.

Isaiah 40:31 NIV – but those who hope in the LORD will renew their strength. They will soar on wings like eagles; they will run and not grow weary, they will walk and not be faint.

Romans 15:13 NIV – May the God of hope fill you with all joy and peace as you trust in him, so that you may over-flow with hope by the power of the Holy Spirit.

Psalm 62:5 NIV – Yes, my soul, find rest in God; my hope comes from him.

Psalm 119:74 NIV – May those who fear you rejoice when they see me, for I have put my hope in your word.

Psalm 25:3 NIV – No one who hopes in you will ever be put to shame, but shame will come on those who are treacherous without excuse.

Psalm 33:17 NIV – A horse is a vain hope for deliverance; despite all its great strength it cannot save.

Psalm 42:5 NIV – Why, my soul, are you downcast? Why so disturbed within me? Put your hope in God, for I will yet praise him, my Savior and my God.

Psalm 130:5 NIV – I wait for the LORD, my whole being waits, and in his word I put my hope.

Psalm 130:7 NIV – Israel, put your hope in the LORD, for with the LORD is unfailing love and with him is full redemption.

Proverbs 13:12 NIV – Hope deferred makes the heart sick, but a longing fulfilled is a tree of life.

Proverbs 23:18 NIV – There is surely a future hope for you, and your hope will not be cut off.

Lamentations 3:21 NIV – Yet this I call to mind and therefore I have hope.

Zechariah 9:12 NIV – Return to your fortress, you prisoners of hope; even now I announce that I will restore twice as much to you.

Jeremiah 29:11 NIV – "For I know the plans I have for you," declares the LORD, "plans to prosper you and not to harm you, plans to give you hope and a future."

Romans 5:2-4 NIV – through whom we have gained access by faith into this grace in which we now stand. And we rejoice in the hope of the glory of God. Not only so, but we also rejoice in our sufferings, because we know that suffering produces perseverance; perseverance, character; and character, hope.

Romans 5:5 NIV – And hope does not put us to shame, because God's love has been poured out into our hearts through the Holy Spirit, who has been given to us.

Romans 8:24-25 NIV – For in this hope we were saved. But hope that is seen is no hope at all. Who hopes for what they already have? But if we hope for what we do not yet have, we wait for it patiently.

Romans 12:12 NIV – Be joyful in hope, patient in affliction, faithful in prayer.

Romans 15:4 NIV – For everything that was written in the past was written to teach us, so that through the endurance taught in the Scriptures and the encouragement they provide we might have hope.

Colossians 1:27 NIV – To them God has chosen to make known among the Gentiles the glorious riches of this mystery, which is Christ in you, the hope of glory.

1 Thessalonians 1:3 NIV – We remember before our God and Father your work produced by faith, your labor prompted by love, and your endurance inspired by hope in our Lord Jesus Christ.

1 Thessalonians 5:8 NIV – But since we belong to the day, let us be sober [self-controlled], putting on faith and love as a breastplate, and the hope of salvation as a helmet.

Titus 1:2 NIV – in the hope of eternal life, which God, who does not lie, promised before the beginning of time.

Hebrews 6:17-18 NIV – Because God wanted to make the unchanging nature of his purpose very clear to the heirs of what was promised, he confirmed it with an oath. God did this so that, by two unchangeable things in which it is impossible for God to lie, we who have fled to take hold of the hope offered to us may be greatly encouraged.

Hebrews 6:19-20 NIV – We have this hope as an anchor for the soul, firm and secure. It enters the inner sanctuary behind the curtain, where our forerunner, Jesus, has entered on our behalf. He has become a high priest forever, in the order of Melchizedek.

Hebrews 10:23 NIV – Let us hold unswervingly to the hope we profess, for he who promised is faithful.

Hebrews 11:1 NIV – Now faith is confidence in what we hope for and assurance about what we do not see.

Romans 8:19-20 NIV – The creation waits in eager expectation for the children of God to be revealed. For the creation was subjected to frustration, not by its own choice, but by the will of the one who subjected it, in hope.

Hebrews 6:11-12 NIV – We want each of you to show this same diligence to the very end, so that what you hope for may be fully realized. We do not want you to become lazy, but to imitate those who through faith and patience inherit what has been promised.

PEACE AND COMFORT SCRIPTURES

Psalm 46:1 – God is our refuge and strength, always ready to help in times of trouble.

Romans 4:20-21 – Abraham never wavered in believing God's promise. In fact, his faith grew stronger, and in this he brought glory to God. He was fully convinced that God is able to do whatever he promises.

Psalm 23 – The Lord is my shepherd; I have all that I need. He lets me rest in green meadows; he leads me beside peaceful streams. He renews my strength. He guides me along right paths, bringing honor to his name. Even when I walk through the darkest valley, I will not be afraid, for you are close beside me. Your rod and your staff protect and comfort me. You prepare a feast for me in the presence of my enemies. You honor me by anointing my head with oil. My cup overflows with blessings. Surely your goodness and unfailing love will pursue me all the days of my life, and I will live in the house of the Lord forever.

John 14:27 – I [Jesus] am leaving you with a gift—peace of mind and heart. And the peace I give is a gift the world cannot give. So don't be troubled or afraid.

Psalm 42:11 – Why am I discouraged? Why is my heart so sad? I will put my hope in God! I will praise him again—my Savior and my God!

Psalm 37:1-5 – Don't worry about the wicked or envy those who do wrong. For like grass, they soon fade away. Like spring flowers, they soon wither. Trust in the Lord and do good. Then you will live safely in the land and prosper. Take delight in the Lord, and he will give you your heart's desires. Commit everything you do to the Lord. Trust him, and he will help you.

Psalm 119:50 NIV – My comfort in my suffering is this: Your promise preserves my life.

Matthew 6:33 NIV – Seek first his kingdom and his righteousness, and all these things will be given to you as well.

Psalm 73:25-26 NIV – Whom have I in heaven but you? And earth has nothing I desire besides you. My flesh and my heart may fail, but God is the strength of my heart and my portion forever.

John 16:33 NIV – I have told you these things, so that in me you may have peace. In this world you will have trouble. But take heart! I have overcome the world.

Isaiah 26:3 NIV – You will keep in perfect peace those whose minds are steadfast, because they trust in you.

2 Thessalonians 3:3 NIV – The Lord is faithful, and he will strengthen and protect you from the evil one.

Philippians 4:6-7 NIV – Do not be anxious about anything, but in every situation, by prayer and petition, with thanksgiving, present your requests to God. And the peace of God, which transcends all understanding, will guard your hearts and your minds in Christ Jesus.

1 Peter 5:6-7 NIV – Humble yourselves, therefore, under God's mighty hand, that he may lift you up in due time. Cast all your anxiety on him because he cares for you.

Psalm 147:3 NIV – He heals the brokenhearted and binds up their wounds.

Ephesians 3:16-17 NIV – I pray that out of His glorious riches He may strengthen you with power through his Spirit in your inner being, so that Christ may dwell in your hearts through faith. And I pray that you, being rooted and established in love…

2 Thessalonians 3:5 NIV – May the Lord direct your hearts into God's love and Christ's perseverance.

2 Thessalonians 2:16-17 NIV – May our Lord Jesus Christ himself and God our Father, who loved us and by his grace gave us eternal encouragement and good hope, encourage your hearts and strengthen you in every good deed and word.

2 Thessalonians 3:16 NIV – May the Lord of peace himself give you peace at all times and in every way. The Lord be with all of you.

SCRIPTURES FOR ENCOURAGEMENT

1 Samuel 12:16 NKJV – stand and see this great thing which the Lord will do before your eyes.

Luke 18:27 NKJV – The things which are impossible with men are possible with God.

Numbers 23:19 NKJV – God is not a man, that He should lie, nor a son of man, that He should repent. Has He said, and will He not do? Or has He spoken, and will He not make it good?

James 1:4 – But let patience have its perfect work, that you may be perfect and complete, lacking nothing.

Romans 8:31 NKJV – ...If God is for us, who can be against us?

2 Timothy 2:1 NKJV – ...be strong in the grace that is in Christ Jesus.

2 Timothy 1:13 NKJV – Hold fast the pattern of sound words...in faith and love...

Colossians 3:2 NKJV – Set your mind on things above, not on things on the earth.

Colossians 3:23 NKJV – Whatever you do, do it heartily, as to the Lord and not to men.

Mark 9:23 NKJV – ...If you can believe, all things are possible to him who believes.

Joshua 1:9 NKJV – ...Be strong and of good courage; do not be afraid, nor be dismayed, for the Lord your God is with you wherever you go.

1 Chronicles 22:18 NKJV – ...And has He not given you rest on every side?...

2 Chronicles 20:17 NKJV – You will not need to fight this battle. Position yourselves, stand still and see the salvation of the Lord, who is with you…

John 16:33 NKJV – …In the world you will have tribulation; but be of good cheer, I have overcome the world.

Romans 8:18 NKJV – For I consider that the sufferings of this present time are not worthy to be compared with the glory which shall be revealed in us.

Romans 8:37 NKJV – Yet in all these things, we are more than conquerors through Him who loved us.

Romans 8:39 NKJV – …[Nothing can] separate us from the love of God which is in Christ Jesus our Lord.

Romans 8:28 NKJV – And we know that all things work together for good to those who love God, to those who are the called according to His purpose.

2 Timothy 4:5 NKJV – But you be watchful in all things, endure afflictions, do the work of an evangelist, fulfill your ministry.

2 Timothy 4:7 NKJV – Fight the good fight, finish the race, keep the faith (paraphrased).

Micah 7:8 NKJV – Do not rejoice over me, my enemy; when I fall, I will arise; when I sit in darkness, the Lord will be a light to me.

Philippians 4:13 – I can do all things through Christ who strengthens me.

1 John 4:4 NKJV – …[You] have overcome them, because He who is in you is greater than he who is in the world.

Philippians 1:6 NKJV – [Be] confident of this very thing, that He who has begun a good work in you will complete it until the day of Jesus Christ.

Philippians 4:4 NKJV – Rejoice in the Lord always. Again I say, rejoice!

SCRIPTURES ON FAITH

1 Peter 5:7 – Give all of your worries and cares to God, for he cares about you.

John 14:27 – I am leaving you with a gift—peace of mind and heart. And the peace I give is a gift the world cannot give. So don't be troubled or afraid.

Philippians 4:6-7 – Don't worry about anything; instead, pray about everything. Tell God what you need, and thank Him for all he has done. Then you will experience God's peace, which exceeds anything we can understand. His peace will guard your hearts and minds as you live in Christ Jesus.

Psalm 40:1-3 – I waited patiently for the Lord to help me, and he turned to me and heard my cry. He lifted me out of the pit of despair, out of the mud and the mire. He set my feet on solid ground and steadied me as I walked along. He has given me a new song to sing, a hymn of praise to our God. Many will see what he has done and be amazed. They will put their trust in the Lord.

Psalm 34:17-19 – The Lord hears his people when they call to him for help. He rescues them from all their troubles. The Lord is close to the brokenhearted; he rescues those whose spirits are crushed. The righteous person faces many troubles, but the Lord comes to the rescue each time.

Isaiah 40:31 – But those who trust in the Lord will find new strength. They will soar high on wings like eagles. They will run and not grow weary. They will walk and not faint.

John 14:1-3 – Don't let your hearts be troubled. Trust in God, and trust also in me. There is more than enough room in my Father's home. If this were not so, would I have told you that I am going to prepare a place for you? When everything is ready, I will come and get you, so that you will always be with me where I am.

Deuteronomy 31:6 – So be strong and courageous! Do not be afraid and do not panic before them. For the Lord your God will personally go ahead of you. He will neither fail you nor abandon you.

Isaiah 41:10 – Don't be afraid, for I am with you. Don't be discouraged, for I am your God. I will strengthen you and help you. I will hold you up with my victorious right hand.

Psalm 112:6-8 – Such people will not be overcome by evil. Those who are righteous will be long remembered. They do not fear bad news; they confidently trust the Lord to care for them. They are confident and fearless and can face their foes triumphantly.

Psalm 32:7-9 – For you are my hiding place; you protect me from trouble. You surround me with songs of victory. The Lord says, "I will guide you along the best pathway for your life. I will advise you and watch over you. Do not be like a senseless horse or mule that needs a bit and bridle to keep it under control."

Hebrews 10:35-38 – So do not throw away this confident trust in the Lord. Remember the great reward it brings you! Patient endurance is what you need now, so that you will continue to do God's will. Then you will receive all that he has promised. "For in just a little while, the Coming One will come and not delay. And my righteous ones will live by faith. But I will take no pleasure in anyone who turns away."

Isaiah 26:3-4 – You will keep in perfect peace all who trust in you, all whose thoughts are fixed on you! Trust in the Lord always, for the Lord God is the eternal Rock.

Psalm 37:7 – Be still in the presence of the Lord, and wait patiently for him to act. Don't worry about evil people who prosper or fret about their wicked schemes.

James 5:7-8 – Dear brothers and sisters, be patient as you wait for the Lord's return. Consider the farmers who patiently wait for the rains in the fall and in the spring. They eagerly look for the valuable harvest to ripen. You, too, must be patient. Take courage, for the coming of the Lord is near.

Romans 8:31-32 – What can we ever say to such wonderful things as these? If God is for us, who can ever be against us? Since he did not spare even his own Son for us but gave him up for us all, won't he also give us everything else?

Isaiah 41:13-14 – For I hold you by your right hand—I, the Lord your God. And I say to you, "Don't be afraid. I am here to help you. Though you are a lowly worm, O Jacob, don't be afraid, people of Israel, for I will help you. I am the Lord, your Redeemer. I am the Holy One of Israel."

Hebrews 13:5-7 – Don't love money; be satisfied with what you have. For God has said, "I will never fail you. I will never abandon you." So we can say with confidence, "The Lord is my helper, so I will have no fear. What can mere people do to me?" Remember your leaders who taught you the word of God. Think of all the good that has come from their lives, and follow the example of their faith.

Psalm 4:8 – In peace I will lie down and sleep, for you alone, O Lord, will keep me safe.

Isaiah 54:10 – "For the mountains may move and the hills disappear, but even then my faithful love for you will remain. My covenant of blessing will never be broken," says the Lord, who has mercy on you.

John 14:18 – No, I will not abandon you as orphans—I will come to you.

Proverbs 3:5-6 – Trust in the Lord with all your heart; do not depend on your own understanding. Seek his will in all you do, and he will show you which path to take.

Philippians 4:11-13 – Not that I was ever in need, for I have learned how to be content with whatever I have. I know how to live on almost nothing or with everything. I have learned the secret of living in every situation, whether it is with a full stomach or empty, with plenty or little. For I can do everything through Christ, who gives me strength.

Psalm 37:8-11 – Stop being angry! Turn from your rage! Do not lose your temper—it only leads to harm. For the wicked will be destroyed, but those who trust in the Lord will possess the land. Soon the wicked will disappear.

Though you look for them, they will be gone. The lowly will possess the land and will live in peace and prosperity.

2 Chronicles 20:17 – "But you will not even need to fight. Take your positions; then stand still and watch the Lord's victory. He is with you, O people of Judah and Jerusalem. Do not be afraid or discouraged. Go out against them tomorrow, for the Lord is with you"

Romans 8:24-25 – We were given this hope when we were saved. (If we already have something, we don't need to hope for it. But if we look forward to something we don't yet have, we must wait patiently and confidently.)

Romans 8:28 – And we know that God causes everything to work together for the good of those who love God and are called according to his purpose for them.

James 1:2-4 – Dear brothers and sisters, when troubles come your way, consider it an opportunity for great joy. For you know that when your faith is tested, your endurance has a chance to grow. So let it grow, for when your endurance is fully developed, you will be perfect and complete, needing nothing.

Habakkuk 2:1 – I will climb up to my watchtower and stand at my guardpost. There I will wait to see what the Lord says and how he will answer my complaint.

Scriptures on Love, Loving, and Being Loved

Matthew 22:36-40 NIV – "Teacher, which is the greatest commandment in the Law?" Jesus replied: "'Love the

Lord your God with all your heart and with all your soul and with all your mind.' This is the first and greatest commandment. And the second is like it: 'Love your neighbor as yourself.' All the Law and the Prophets hang on these two commandments."

Mark 10:21 NIV – Jesus looked at him and loved him. "One thing you lack," he said. "Go, sell everything you have and give to the poor, and you will have treasure in heaven. Then come, follow me."

Luke 6:31-36 NIV – Do to others as you would have them do to you. If you love those who love you, what credit is that to you? Even sinners love those who love them. And if you do good to those who are good to you, what credit is that to you? Even sinners do that. And if you lend to those from whom you expect repayment, what credit is that to you? Even sinners lend to sinners, expecting to be repaid in full. But love your enemies, do good to them, and lend to them without expecting to get anything back. Then your reward will be great, and you will be sons of the Most High, because he is kind to the ungrateful and wicked. Be merciful, just as your Father is merciful.

John 3:16 NIV – For God so loved the world that he gave his one and only Son, that whoever believes in him shall not perish but have eternal life.

John 10:17 NIV – The reason my Father loves me is that I lay down my life—only to take it up again.

John 12:25 NIV – Anyone who loves their life will lose it, while anyone who hates their life in this world will keep it for eternal life.

John 13:1 NIV – It was just before the Passover Festival. Jesus knew that the time had come for him to leave this world and go to the Father. Having loved his own who were in the world, he loved them to the end.

John 13:34-35 NIV – A new command I give you: Love one another. As I have loved you, so you must love one another. By this everyone will know that you are my disciples, if you love one another.

John 14:15 NIV – If you love me, keep my commands.

John 14:21-25 NIV – "Whoever has my commands and keeps them is the one who loves me. The one who loves me will be loved by my Father, and I too will love them and show myself to them." Then Judas (not Judas Iscariot) said, "But, Lord, why do you intend to show yourself to us and not to the world?" Jesus replied, "Anyone who loves me will obey my teaching. My Father will love them, and we will come to them and make our home with them. Anyone who does not love me will not obey my teaching. These words you hear are not my own; they belong to the Father who sent me. All this I have spoken while still with you."

John 15:9-13 NIV – As the Father has loved me, so have I loved you. Now remain in my love. If you keep my commands, you will remain in my love, just as I have kept my Father's commands and remain in his love. I have told you this so that my joy may be in you and that your joy may be complete. My command is this: Love each other as I have loved you. Greater love has no one than this, to lay down one's life for one's friends.

Romans 5:5 NIV – And hope does not put us to shame, because God's love has been poured out into our hearts through the Holy Spirit, who has been given to us.

Romans 5:8 NIV – But God demonstrates his own love for us in this: While we were still sinners, Christ died for us.

Romans 8:28-35 NIV – And we know that in all things God works for the good of those who love him, who have been called according to his purpose. For those God foreknew he also predestined to be conformed to the likeness of his Son, that he might be the firstborn among many brothers and sisters. And those he predestined, he also called; those he called, he also justified; those he justified, he also glorified. What, then, shall we say in response to this? If God is for us, who can be against us? He who did not spare his own Son, but gave him up for us all—how will he not also, along with him, graciously give us all things? Who will bring any charge against those whom God has chosen? It is God who justifies. Who is he that condemns? Christ Jesus, who died—more than that, who was raised to life—is at the right hand of God and is also interceding for us. Who shall separate us from the love of Christ? Shall trouble or hardship or persecution or famine or nakedness or danger or sword?

Romans 12:8-10 NIV – if it is to encourage, then give encouragement; if it is giving, then give generously; if it is to lead, do it diligently; if it is to show mercy, do it cheerfully. Love must be sincere. Hate what is evil; cling to what is good. Be devoted to one another in love. Honor one another above yourselves.

1 Corinthians 2:8-10 NIV – None of the rulers of this age understood it, for if they had, they would not have

crucified the Lord of glory. However, as it is written: "What no eye has seen, what no ear has heard, and what no human mind has conceived"—the things God has prepared for those who love him—these are the things God has revealed to us by his Spirit. The Spirit searches all things, even the deep things of God.

1 Corinthians 13 NIV 1984 – If I speak in the tongues of men and of angels, but have not love, I am only a resounding gong or a clanging cymbal. If I have the gift of prophecy and can fathom all mysteries and all knowledge, and if I have a faith that can move mountains, but have not love, I am nothing. If I give all I possess to the poor and surrender my body to the flames, but have not love, I gain nothing. Love is patient, love is kind. It does not envy, it does not boast, it is not proud. It is not rude, it is not self-seeking, it is not easily angered, it keeps no record of wrongs. Love does not delight in evil but rejoices with the truth. It always protects, always trusts, always hopes, always perseveres. Love never fails. But where there are prophecies, they will cease; where there are tongues, they will be stilled; where there is knowledge, it will pass away. For we know in part and we prophesy in part, but when perfection comes, the imperfect disappears. When I was a child, I talked like a child, I thought like a child, I reasoned like a child. When I became a man, I put childish ways behind me. Now we see but a poor reflection as in a mirror; then we shall see face to face. Now I know in part; then I shall know fully, even as I am fully known. And now these three remain: faith, hope and love. But the greatest of these is love.

1 Corinthians 16:14 NIV – Do everything in love.

2 Corinthians 5:14 NIV – For Christ's love compels us, because we are convinced that one died for all, and therefore all died.

Galatians 2:20 NIV – I have been crucified with Christ and I no longer live, but Christ lives in me. The life I now live in the body, I live by faith in the Son of God, who loved me and gave himself for me.

Galatians 5:13-14 NIV – You, my brothers and sisters, were called to be free. But do not use your freedom to indulge the flesh; rather, serve one another humbly in love. For the entire law is fulfilled in keeping this one command: "Love your neighbor as yourself."

Galatians 5:22-23 NIV – But the fruit of the Spirit is love, joy, peace, forbearance [patience], kindness, goodness, faithfulness, gentleness and self-control. Against such things there is no law.

CONTACT THE AUTHOR

If you would like to contact the author
please email: claudine@tribal.net.au
or call 0417 919 771